A
RADICAL
Enterprise

PRAISE FOR *A RADICAL ENTERPRISE*

"*A Radical Enterprise* is a masterclass on the future of business. Parker inspires us with practical solutions for building open, decentralized organizations and shows us how to create the conditions for teams of any size to find meaning and fulfillment in their work."

—**Aaron Pava**, Chief Experience Officer (CXO),
CivicActions

"This book will challenge you! Matt K. Parker explores the often surprising frontiers of how organizations can run. He looks at thirteen businesses that have chosen to adopt organizational philosophies that may seem alien and strange but when presented with fifty years of scholarly research are suddenly not so crazy after all."

—**Gene Kim**, Author, Researcher, and
Founder of IT Revolution

"Parker has had a front row seat as many organizations sought to empower their teams and become more nimble and effective. He has seen what works and what doesn't. This book will give you the often surprising answers. It turns out that making your organization more powerful depends on senior leaders giving up their power. Parker does a brilliant job explaining why that not only works but is necessary to create more effective and more enjoyable workplaces."

—**Paul Gaffney**, Chief Technology and
Supply Chain Officer, Kohl's

"Management as we know it is a century-old, outdated technology; we need to radically reinvent how we organize and collaborate to rise to the challenges of our time, and this book offers some powerful tools for that journey."

—**Brian J. Robertson**, author of *Holacracy: The New Management
System for a Rapidly Changing World*

"Matt takes years of intuition and learnings from the bleeding edge of hypergrowth software organizations and codifies them in a framework that applies to any knowledge-work business. It's an exciting glimpse into the future of work we should all strive to achieve."

—**Ross Hale**, CEO, Artium

"*A Radical Enterprise* is a very important work and deserves to receive a very wide readership. It is organized around what makes up the foundation of radical collaboration: team autonomy, managerial devolution, deficiency gratification, and candid vulnerability. The author gives many real-world examples of radically collaborative companies practicing these imperatives.

Even after a few years of practicing and studying the field of radical collaboration, I was surprised by some of the statistics. For example, '98% of employees are authentically dedicated, 97% are deeply accountable, and 97% are fully responsible for their work and actions.'

What I found most refreshing about this book is that it speaks to what is key and important to becoming a radically collaborative workplace and producing tangible results. And it's about how our world is going to metamorphosize from a system of domination to one of collaboration. Kudos to Matt Parker!"

—**Matt Perez**, cofounder of Nearsoft and
coauthor of *RADICAL Companies*

Pioneering the Future of
High-Performing Organizations

A
RADICAL
Enterprise

MATT K. PARKER

IT Revolution
Portland, Oregon

25 NW 23rd Pl, Suite 6314
Portland, OR 97210

First Edition
Printed in the United States of America
27 26 25 24 23 22   1 2 3 4 5 6 7 8 9 10

Cover design by Devon Smith Creative
Book design by Devon Smith Creative

Library of Congress Control Number: 2021948594

ISBN: 9781950508006
eBook ISBN: 9781950508020
Kindle ISBN: 9781950508037
Web PDF ISBN: 9781950508044
Audio download: 9781950508013

For information about special discounts for bulk purchases
or for information on booking authors for an event,
please visit our website at www.ITRevolution.com.

A RADICAL ENTERPRISE

CONTENTS

To Charlie, Ruby, and River,
and to the radically collaborative future you may inherit.

PREFACE

Every book begins as an idea, and every idea is born in a time and place. So I guess you could say that this book was born in a basement in the year 2001. At that time, I had just started my first programming internship within the IT department of a major hospital system in Dallas, Texas. On my first day, my manager met me in the lobby and led me to an elevator, which, to my surprise, took us not *up* to where I imagined I would be working but *down* to the basement, where we wound our way through a subterranean maze of flickering fluorescent lights and cinder block corridors until we arrived at an unmarked door that my manager opened while saying, "Welcome to IT."

Behind that unmarked door stood a cramped and dim cubicle farm populated by programmers and IT professionals and lit by the pale glow of terminals. The carpet was gray, as were the chairs and cubes. There were no windows, no plants, no decorations, and, most unsettling of all, no noise save the tap-tap-tapping of fingers on keys and the whirring of a tape archive system emanating from an even deeper chamber within this veritable dungeon.

To say that this environment was oppressive would be an understatement. This was the stereotype we all joke about, the impersonal corporate hierarchy, but here it was made real as it literally and figuratively bore down on the knowledge workers toiling away underground, creating and maintaining the software and systems that the hospitals ran on.

This was where intense and unyielding managers drove impossible deadlines with unrealistic scopes. Where IT professionals suffered long hours in quiet desperation. Where passion, innovation, and creativity were slowly yet unrelentingly drained from the workforce and replaced by disengagement, mistrust, and apathy.

I was young and inexperienced at the time. I knew nothing about the theoretical underpinnings of this way of working or the empirical evidence against its financial efficacy. Nonetheless, I was convinced of three things:

1. This way of working is bad for people.
2. This way of working is bad for business.
3. This way of working is a choice.

That's not to say that I thought this way of working was due to the choice of any one individual. Rather, I intuited that nothing about this way of structuring and organizing knowledge work was necessary.

It is not individual choice but the collective sum of present and past choices that has resulted in this self-replicating system of work that dehumanizes people, sabotages organizational performance, and diminishes creativity and innovation. We have collectively taken a world so filled with the potential for joy, fulfillment, and meaning and replaced it with an encumbrance of stress and strife. What I guessed then but now *know* is that we can make any sort of world we want, if only we disentangle ourselves from the historical morass that we have all inherited and find a new path forward for human sociality.

Of course, back in 2001 I had no idea what that new path might look like, so I spent the next ten long years working in a series of dehumanizing environments until a small but reputable consulting company, Pivotal Labs, invited me to interview with them. I had used their opinionated product management software, Pivotal Tracker, for years, but I knew next to nothing about how Pivotal Labs actually worked. Since I was employed by a large hierarchical enterprise at the time, in which the daily experience of work was akin to swimming upstream through a river of mud, I jumped at the opportunity to interview somewhere else.

I'll never forget my first impressions of Pivotal Labs. Back then, their New York office was a single open floor—a tumbling sea of sitting and standing desks. Each desk had one computer but two developers programming together by passing control of the keyboard and mouse back and forth. I had heard of "pair programming" before, but I had never seen it and had certainly never imagined it at this scale. The sight of so many pairs was staggering—and so was the *sound*.

It was loud. All the pairs were talking. They were discussing, debating, and debugging their code all at once and in the most animated tones, resulting in a dazzling mixture of passion, humility, fascination, and frustration swirling about the room.

But there was something more about this situation that impressed upon me. Something unexpected. At first I couldn't quite place what it was, but then it hit me: they were *smiling*. There were literally *so many smiles* in the room. I had spent so long working within a demoralizing environment of domination and coercion that the experience of seeing joy at work was uncanny.

Needless to say, I took the job. I spent the next decade working for Pivotal Labs. I learned the ins and outs of Extreme Programming, Lean product development, and human-centered design. I played a variety of roles, including consultant, manager, director, and global head of engineering.

On teams, I experienced a sense of partnership and equality that I had never known in previous jobs. Instead of disengagement and mistrust, I found passion and belongingness. Instead of politics and control, I found candor and vulnerability. Joy, meaning, purpose, fulfillment—all of these qualities became possible, if not always attainable, while I was there.

Unfortunately, this state of affairs didn't last. Thanks to a series of acquisitions, Pivotal Labs struggled to maintain a culture of radical collaboration over the intervening years. It increasingly adopted elements of traditional corporate hierarchies until it was eventually acquired and dissolved by a hierarchical behemoth. Nonetheless, I am still thankful for my time there and for all that it taught me. It gave me hope that a better world is possible, and it even gave me a small glimpse into what it might take to get there.

I have since been inspired to find organizations that eschew command-and-control dynamics for partnership and equality; that buck the trend toward disengagement and mistrust and replace it with joy, meaning, and fulfillment; that leverage the power of self-management and intrinsic motivation to scale their social and economic impact within the world. I have scoured the globe looking for these organizations. And I have found them. Not just a few here and there. A whole host of them, including some massive, world-shaking, industry-dominating giants.

I've discovered that what is good for people is also good for corporations. That the paradigms of partnership and equality don't just lead to individual growth and personal fulfillment—they also lead to organizational performance and economic superiority.

Here in this book, I have detailed the experiences and practices of radically collaborative organizations and distilled their essence into four imperatives for you to learn: *team autonomy*, *managerial devolution*, *deficiency gratification*, and *candid vulnerability*.

I'm not claiming that what follows constitutes an exact blueprint for changing your organization. I'm not even claiming that I've invented anything here. My work stands on the shoulders of giants, both in industry and in academia. But by synthesizing the concrete experiences of radically collaborative organizations together with the multidisciplinary theories that help explain their success, I believe this book will give readers a tremendous leg up in any radically collaborative transformation. That's because the structures, practices, concepts, and ideas found within these pages can be applied at multiple levels and junctures.

Radical collaboration can transform the way we structure global socioeconomic systems, but it can also transform the way we relate to each other, one on one. We can use it to restructure organizations through partnership and equality—and we can also use it to restructure conversations through candor and vulnerability. Autonomy, self-management, performance, innovation—these are all concepts and outcomes within the domain of radical collaboration that we can immediately run with, whether we are a CEO or an individual contributor.

And run with them we must. Although the path to radical collaboration may not always be easy or straight, I believe that the journey is an existential imperative. As the following pages of this book will make plain, the traditional world of work is in crisis. Performance and productivity have been stagnating for decades. Workers are experiencing unprecedented levels of disengagement, mistrust, and meaninglessness, with devastating economic consequences.

And now here, in the midst of the COVID-19 pandemic, they're quitting their jobs in droves. We have reached an inflection point, and we have a choice to make. Either we continue to choose the old organizational and cultural paradigms that have resulted in so much of our socioeconomic hardships and privations or we choose the paradigms of partnership and equality that lead to superior organizational performance and individual joy, meaning, fulfillment, and actualization.

I have made my choice. And if you're reading this book, then I'll wager you've made your choice too. So let us, you and I, turn the page and take our first steps toward a better world. Together. Collaboratively. *Radically*.

INTRODUCTION

It's summer 2021. COVID-19 vaccinations have already reached a majority of American adults. Summer camps have reopened; schools are preparing for full, in-person enrollment in the fall; and businesses and governments are heralding a "return to normal." Yet a quick glance at the articles of any major American news outlet paints a troubling picture.

A study by the Harvard Business School found that over 80% of workers don't want to go back to the office full time,[1] while a similar study from the global data intelligence company Morning Consult found that 40% of workers would rather quit than go back to the office full time.[2]

Researchers at the global jobs site Monster.com found that "a whopping 95% of workers are considering changing jobs, and 92% are even willing to switch industries to find the right position"—a shift driven, at least in part, by "burnout and lack of growth opportunities."[3]

In April 2021, nearly four million Americans voluntarily quit their jobs—"the highest monthly number ever reported by the US Bureau of Labor Statistics," according to the *Dallas Morning News*.[4]

Yet, despite high unemployment, the US is experiencing critical labor shortages, with businesses from "the biggest metropolitan areas and from small towns" reporting a "catastrophic inability to hire."[5]

For the first time in history, a vast cross-section of workers are leaving the workforce en masse, leading the American economy to face an unprecedented crisis of *voluntary* unemployment that economists have dubbed "The Great Resignation."[6]

For some industries, like hospitality, this phenomenon was predictable. As the *New York Times* reports, unemployment insurance and pandemic relief benefits often rival the former income of many hospitality workers, like waiters and cooks.[7] Why go back to a job marked by low wages, long hours, and high stress—not to mention dangerous working conditions due to COVID-19—when you can make just as much money staying home, staying safe, and spending more time with your family? Or, as many of these former hospitality workers have done, why not choose to pursue a career in construction, commercial trucking, or even retail, where education requirements are commensurate yet wages are higher?

But what is perhaps less expected is that many highly paid knowledge workers—like programmers, designers, and product managers—are also quitting their jobs rather than go back to their offices. Although the popular image of the white-collar knowledge worker includes high salaries, nine-to-five hours, and cushy benefits, the reality is that even before the pandemic, knowledge workers were plagued by long hours and "always on" expectations from managers, leading to high levels of burnout and stress, which has only worsened during the pandemic.[8]

According to a report from Indeed.com, "Employee burnout has only gotten worse over the last year: more than half (52%) of respondents are feeling burned out, and more than two-thirds (67%) believe the feeling has worsened over the course of the pandemic."[9]

At the same time, with their offices closed and their bosses physically removed, knowledge workers have experienced greater autonomy in their jobs and greater flexibility in their lives. Many have chosen to ditch a strict nine-to-five schedule, preferring to shift their hours or spread their work tasks out throughout the day to achieve a better work/life balance (a factor that 83% of millennials rate as their number-one consideration in their jobs).[10] Others have taken their laptops into their backyards, to a park bench, or even to a beach, allowing them to take advantage of the significant physical and mental health benefits of being outside that scientists have recently validated and quantified.[11]

According to an article from Yale Environment 360,

> In a study of 20,000 people, a team led by Mathew White of the European Centre for Environment & Human Health at the University of Exeter, found that people who spent two hours a week in green spaces—local parks or other natural environments, either all at once or spaced over several visits—were substantially more likely to report good health and psychological well-being than those who don't. . . .
>
> These studies have shown that time in nature—as long as people feel safe—is an antidote for stress: It can lower blood pressure and stress hormone levels, reduce nervous system arousal, enhance immune system function, increase self-esteem, reduce anxiety, and improve mood.[12]

Lastly, with less managerial oversight or interference, many knowledge workers have collaborated more freely with their peers—spending less time in large meetings and more time deciding among themselves what to do and how and when to do it.[13]

According to a recent report from *Harvard Business Review*,

> Researchers studied knowledge workers in 2013 and again during the 2020 pandemic lockdown and found significant changes in how they are working. They learned that lockdown helps people focus on the tasks that really matter. They spent 12% less time drawn into large meetings and 9% more time interacting with customers and external partners. Lockdown also helped people take responsibility for our own schedules. They did 50% more activities through personal choice and half as many because someone else asked them to. Finally, during lockdown, people viewed their work as more worthwhile. The number of tasks rated as tiresome dropped from 27% to 12%, and the number we could readily offload to others dropped from 41% to 27%.[14]

So, as vaccinations roll out and as exasperated business owners clamor for a return to the office, knowledge workers have begun to ask themselves: "What do I stand to gain by going back—and what do I stand to lose?"

Dominator Hierarchies

The answer to that question depends primarily on the nature of the organization that they work for. Unfortunately, the majority of them work within an organizational structure that precipitated "The Great Resignation"—a structure that business leaders often hint at through euphemisms like "command and control," "bureaucracy," and "Taylorism" but that sociologists baldly refer to as "dominator hierarchies."

Dr. Riane Eisler—the world-renowned social scientist who introduced the concept of dominator hierarchies in her bestselling book *The Chalice and the Blade*—writes that the dominator model

> . . . organize[s] relationships at all levels according to a hierarchy of control, status, and privilege. [It extends] rights and freedoms to those on top and denies them to those on the bottom. Such rankings lead to thinking limited to two dimensions: superior or inferior;

dominating or dominated. . . . Both parties live in fear. Those on top fear loss of power and control while those on the bottom perpetually seek to gain it.[15]

A significant corollary of a dominator hierarchy is coercion. As Dr. Eisler writes, "behaviors, attitudes, and perceptions that do not conform to dominator norms are systematically discouraged . . . directly, through personal coercion, and indirectly, through intermittent social shows of force."[16]

Today, most businesses are characterized by a dominator hierarchy—by a rank ordering of people, with power and resources distributed unequally and concentrated at the top. The judgments of the dominators—the bosses, managers, "leaders," etc.—are structurally privileged over and above the judgments of the dominated. This power of judgement is conferred upon dominators through subjective and ultimately arbitrary promotion processes. And it is wielded by coercion—by explicit and implicit threats.

Explicit threats include "Do this or you're fired," while implicit threats include modern management techniques like performance evaluations, annual goal-setting exercises, pay-for-performance schemes, and performance improvement plans. Thanks to these techniques, your boss can "ask" you to do things with a smile, leaving unstated and implicit the consequences for not doing as you were "asked" to do.

As a method of corporate organization, dominator hierarchies can be traced back to the Industrial Revolution, where attempts to rapidly increase the production of manufactured products led to a system of domination and coercion euphemistically referred to as *scientific management*, in which workers were reduced to replaceable cogs, or living machines, and made to be ordered about and controlled under strict specifications.

Although this paradigm is unjustifiable from the standpoint of any humanistic value system, and although it is unnecessary and even disadvantageous with respect to the demands of mass production (as we will see later in this book when we encounter radically collaborative manufacturing methods that enhance both individual well-being and organizational performance), it is at least easy to see why factory owners were so quick to embrace dominator hierarchies.

Manufacturers were in the business of producing specific quantities of fixed products with precise specifications via purpose-made machinery. With all variables known and relatively unchanging, the coordination of many roles could be fully planned and specified up front and then controlled and optimized like some vast biological machine. Although the results were dehumanizing, the rationale is at least explainable.

However, this same scheme of sociality loses all semblance of rationality when applied to knowledge work. Unlike manufacturing, knowledge work explicitly and squarely falls within the domain of the unknown. Knowledge workers, like programmers, are solving problems and creating knowledge products for a user base that is fundamentally dynamic; whose needs, wants, and desires are forever shifting in unpredictable ways, and who exist in a rapidly evolving technology landscape that is radically reshaping the way human beings interrelate to each other on a broad social scale.

To take a paradigm of social organization that attempts to optimize output based on static quantities and controlled variables and apply it to a domain that is inherently creative and unpredictable is a recipe for disaster. And yet that is exactly what we have done.

The Great Resignation

"The Great Resignation" is not the transient effect of a new dynamic but the end result of a great malaise that has been gaining momentum over the past century. As the vast majority of knowledge workers have been irrationally corralled into a paradigm of domination and coercion, we have barreled head-first into a striking socioeconomic crisis with dire consequences for individuals and corporations alike, including:

Disengagement: Engagement at work is defined as a state of mind characterized by "vigor, dedication, and absorption"[17]— clearly something all organizations should strive for. Yet a 2018 global study found that only 16% of workers feel engaged at work. The other 84% feel disengaged—unenthusiastic about the company's mission, unsupported by their team and their leaders, and unrecognized for their unique talents.[18] Even more disconcerting, among those that feel disengaged, 18% are *actively* disengaged. According to the research and management consulting organization Gallup, "Actively disengaged employees aren't just unhappy at work—they are resentful that their needs aren't being met and are acting out their unhappiness. Every day, these workers potentially undermine what their engaged coworkers accomplish."[19]

Gallup estimates the global costs of disengagement at a staggering $7 trillion per year in lost productivity.[20]

Mistrust: Mistrust is rampant in the world. According to the 2021 Edelman Trust Barometer, people mistrust institutions at unprecedented levels.[21] Years of misinformation, a global pandemic, and extreme economic instability have led to a crisis of trust in governments, NGOs, the media, and yes, businesses too. Employee trust in business leaders is at an all-time low. In France, for instance, only 22% of people trust their CEO, while in Japan that number drops to just 18%. And globally, 56% of people feel that "business leaders are *purposely* trying to mislead people by saying things they know are false or gross exaggerations."[22] A lack of trust in the workplace has significant economic consequences, as researchers have found that high-trust workplace environments lead to eleven times more innovation and six times more organizational performance.[23]

Meaninglessness: Most people just don't find work within a dominator hierarchy meaningful. In fact, the 2018 study "Meaning and Purpose at Work" found that nine out of ten people find their work *so* meaningless that they would be willing to exchange a whopping 23% of their entire future lifetime earnings for more meaningful work.[24] Since that amount is more than the average worker spends on housing in their lifetime, the authors of the study suggest that it might be time to update the list of human essentials for the twenty-first century to "food, clothing, shelter—and meaningful work."[25]

Disengagement, mistrust, and meaninglessness are just three of the disaffecting traits of dominator hierarchies, with their attendant economic consequences. But the list goes on. For example, dominator hierarchies lead to high levels of job insecurity among workers—which researchers have found to reduce productivity[26] and to significantly increase the risk of mental and physical health disorders.[27] Dominator hierarchies also diminish critical thinking; researchers have found that our ability to ask why and to question the judgments of others is inversely proportional to the amount of domination and authority that we are subjected to.[28] And lastly, dominator hierarchies are marked by high levels of employee turnover[29]—a troubling fact given that replacing a worker who quits can, by one conservative estimate, cost twice that worker's annual salary.[30]

In light of all of this, it's easy to see why so many knowledge workers have resisted returning to their offices or have quit their jobs altogether now that they've glimpsed a new way of working based on trust and autonomy and have gained some measure of control over the what, where, when, and how of their work. Instead of taking a step back to "normal," they want to take two steps forward toward a radically new way of doing business that gives them the autonomy, trust, and esteem that they need and deserve—and they're willing to quit their jobs to get there.

Our Dominator Hierarchy Inheritance

I'll pause here to highlight that the business architectures and dynamics that knowledge workers work in today are, for the most part, inherited. Most business leaders set out to build companies, not dominator hierarchies. They are focused on explicit ideas for products and services, not tacit paradigms like domination and coercion. When they wind up structuring their organization as a dominator hierarchy, few of them do so by conscious choice; rather, they're just "going with the flow."

Dominator hierarchies naturally form, and naturally replicate, because for most of us, that's all we've ever known. We have been organizing work this way since at least the Industrial Revolution. It's the implicit structure taught in almost every business school as the best (and really only) way to organize and manage a business. And yet it has led businesses all over the world to fail to meet the needs of the socioeconomic environments that they inhabit. The disaffecting ills that we now find ourselves immersed in have been coming for a long time—the COVID-19 pandemic simply brought them to a head faster.

It's also important to note that a great many business leaders are not only aware of the ills that plague their corporations, they're actively attempting to mitigate them by creating better cultures and governance within their organizations. They are creating programs for diversity, equity, and inclusion; conducting training in psychological safety; and inventing practices like blameless postmortems and OKRs (objectives and key results).

These leaders are doing the very hard and very necessary work to overcome some of the most damaging effects and inequalities that we have all inherited from centuries of domination and coercion. The intent of this book is not to criticize any of these leaders or their efforts. Rather, the intention is to support them by asking all of us, collectively, to take this process one step further.

So long as we are attempting to mitigate individual disaffection and organizational inefficacy while doing nothing to change the underlying organizational paradigm that these ills stem from, we are addressing symptoms, not causes. It's like a community trying to clean up a dirty river while doing nothing about the factory upstream pumping waste into it. We can sift debris out of the river all day long, but at some point we're all going to have to wade upstream and figure out how to solve the problem at its source.

Radical Collaboration: Pioneering a New Organizational Future

Thankfully, knowledge workers and business leaders don't have to start from scratch. Over the past few decades, a small but growing percentage of corporations have pioneered a new way of working founded on partnership and equality instead of domination and coercion. A way of working that is, as Dr. Eisler puts it, "based on the principle of linking rather than ranking"[31]—where static dominator hierarchies, managers, and bureaucracies are jettisoned in favor of dynamic, self-managing, *self-linking* networks of teams. As we'll see shortly, these organizations feature a radical approach to collaboration, grounded in the intrinsic motivation of the participants and formed through the freely given commitments of peers. For that reason, we'll refer to these organizations as *radically collaborative*.

The body of this book illustrates, through stories and research, the four imperatives of radically collaborative organizations: team autonomy, managerial devolution, deficiency gratification, and candid vulnerability.

These are the modern business dynamics that will allow companies of all sizes and across all industries to outperform, out-innovate, and out-engage the competition in the marketplace.

If you're reading this book, chances are you have already decided that something needs to change in the worker/business relationship. You're already aware that if nothing changes, the consequences could very well be catastrophic. For knowledge workers, this seems to be an obvious conclusion. Yet most businesses are balking. Their biggest concern is often not how to change but why change at all. Dominator hierarchies, for the most part, seem to be working out well for shareholders (even if not for all the stakeholders). So why risk rocking the fiscal boat?

I'll tell you why. *Because the boat is already rocking.* Radically collaborative organizations aren't just sitting around playing nice. They're coming for you. In fact, they're already here, comprising 8% of the world's corporations[32]—and that number is rapidly growing. They are disrupting industries and captivating customers by outperforming traditional enterprises on practically every economic dimension. Three of the largest and most successful radically collaborative organizations changing the world today are Haier, Morning Star, and Buurtzorg.

Haier: Radical Collaboration through Microenterprises

AT A GLANCE

Haier: Number one appliance manufacturer in the world. Eighty-thousand people. Founded in 1920. Notable for the radically collaborative structure of self-managing microenterprises..

Haier is an appliance manufacturer and pioneer of the Internet of Things based in China, with annual revenues in excess of $38 billion. It's the global leader in appliances, ranking number one in retail sales value for eleven consecutive years.[33] It's a pioneer in smart-home technology and services, and it has also successfully branched out into dozens of other industries as diverse as video gaming, cattle ranching, and health care.[34] Its new ventures total over $2 billion in market valuation, while its core appliance business has seen 22% year-over-year growth in gross profit over the last decade.[35]

Haier has achieved all of this through a self-organizing company structure composed of thousands of tiny "microenterprises." These microenterprises are autonomous, entrepreneurial mini-companies typically consisting of ten to fifteen people. Each has its own purpose, product or service, and profit-and-loss statement. At Haier, there are no middle managers, no labyrinth of procedures, and no soul-crushing red tape. Instead, microenterprises set their own goals and targets, make their own plans, and freely relate to each other as they please.

The Xinchu microenterprise, for example, creates a smart-home refrigerator that seamlessly connects users to third-party grocery delivery services.[36] To develop and deliver this product, Xinchu purchases services from other Haier microenterprises that provide services like manufacturing and marketing. But Xinchu has also contracted with organizations outside the company for goods and services—sometimes because there was no equivalent internal microenterprise and sometimes because they believed that an outside organization could provide better value than an internal microenterprise.[37]

Each microenterprise may choose who to purchase services from without approval or oversight because, as Haier's CEO Zhang Ruimin believes, "trade-offs are best made by those closest to the customer—by microenterprises that are free to choose when to collaborate and when to go it alone."[38] By pushing decision-making power out of dominator hierarchies and into a decentralized swarm of radically collaborative microenterprises, Haier can experiment, evolve, and innovate like few others in the world.

Ruimin is inspired by the ancient Chinese text *I Ching*, which likens the highest stage of human development to a "host of dragons without a leader"—an image he says is an apt metaphor for Haier itself:

> In Chinese culture, the dragon is the mightiest animal. Today, each and every microenterprise is a kind of dragon, very capable and competent. But they don't have a leader. They start their own businesses on the market without the guidance of a leader. That is the highest level of human governance.[39]

By focusing on the basic dignity and unrealized potential of every person within the organization, Haier has created a powerful force in the world both for individual fulfillment and for corporate success.

Morning Star: Radical Collaboration with Zero Bosses

AT A GLANCE

Morning Star: Largest tomato processor in the world. One hundred percent self-managing structure re-designed annually through CLOUs (colleague letters of understanding).

Radical collaboration has also found success within the food processing industry. Morning Star, the largest tomato processor in the world, is a radically collaborative organization in which there are zero managers or bosses. Instead of organizing work through a dominator hierarchy, the more than four thousand colleagues start every year by meeting as equals, without any formal roles or titles, and crafting colleague letters of understanding, or CLOUs.[40]

At a microlevel, these CLOUs encapsulate the freely given commitments that colleagues will make to each other that year—i.e., how they will collaborate to take that year's tomato crops and turn them into a processed result, like diced tomatoes or puree. But at a macrolevel, the CLOUs spell out how all of the colleagues will collectively self-manage every aspect of the company that year, from day-to-day food processing to equipment purchasing and payroll.

Before creating Morning Star, Chris Rufer ran his own single-rig trucking company, delivering goods—like tomatoes—to factories. As his colleague Doug Kirkpatrick writes in *The No-Limits Enterprise*, Rufer noticed that "despite the ever-present layers of management, the factories where he delivered his loads were mostly inefficient and poorly run. He was convinced that pointless bureaucracy was behind much of the ineffectiveness and disengagement that he saw."[41]

His solution? "Rufer decided that Morning Star should have no levels of management. Just as they did in the outside world, the company's colleagues (who formerly would have been called 'employees') would manage *themselves* as they moved through negotiated commitments to their colleagues and to the enterprise as a whole."[42]

Although many called him crazy at the time, it's hard to argue with the results. Since founding the company in 1990, Morning Star has become the largest tomato processor in the world by volume[43] and is responsible for a full 40% of America's tomato paste and diced tomato products alone.[44] And they've done all of this without bosses, managers, or any of the hierarchical trappings that we've come to expect from corporations today.

Buurtzorg: Radical Collaboration through Self-Organizing Teams

AT A GLANCE

Buurtzorg: Number one home health-care provider in the Netherlands. Fifteen-thousand colleagues. Broken into thousands of small, self-managing teams.

Radical collaboration is taking the field of health care by storm too. Consider the Dutch not-for-profit company Buurtzorg (a Dutch word for "neighborhood care") that provides in-home care to the sick and the elderly. The organization currently consists of eleven thousand nurses and four thousand domestic helpers.[45]

Like Haier, the fifteen thousand professionals are divided into thousands of small, self-managing teams consisting of ten to twelve nurses each, and each team covers a specific geographic area.[46] Without managers, hierarchies, or bureaucracies, each team is responsible for finding clients, renting facilities, recruiting new hires, scheduling work, and managing budgets.[47] Every member of the team is a client-facing nurse but, in addition to their nursing work, they each take turns playing various roles, like treasurer, planner, and mentor[48]—in effect, turning management into a shared and dynamic responsibility instead of the purview of a static hierarchy.

In the short time since Buurtzorg was founded in 2006, they've already taken over the home health-care industry in the Netherlands, employing "60% of community nurses" there (many of whom fled their hierarchical competitors to join them).[49] They've also expanded into twenty-five other countries, including Sweden, Japan, and the United States.

Their rapid growth is at least partially explained by their results: Buurtzorg patients are on average 30% more satisfied with their care as compared to the care provided by Buurtzorg's for-profit competitors.[50] And they are 33% less likely to be admitted to a hospital[51]—a testament to the consistency and quality of care that Buurtzorg's nurses provide.

Data Supporting Radically Collaborative Organizations

Haier, Morning Star, and Buurtzorg are the vanguard for a small but growing contingent of radically collaborative organizations disrupting businesses around the world.

The 2016 *HOW Report* from the Legal Research Network, with support from the University of Southern California and the Boston Research Group, studied the sentiments of sixteen thousand workers across seventeen countries and found that three classifications of organizations emerged, with one class clearly outperforming the rest.[52]

The first category of organization is referred to as "blind obedience." Businesses that fall into this category exhibit the most obvious and ruthless forms of dominator hierarchies. Within these organizations, what the boss says goes—or else.

The second class is called "informed acquiescence." These businesses are also structured as dominator hierarchies but have softened their overall perception through the adoption of twentieth-century "good management" practices like performance evaluations and annual goal exercises.

The last, smallest, yet highest-performing class of organization is referred to as "self-governing" (what will be called "radically collaborative" throughout this book). According to the *HOW Report*, businesses within this category are "purpose-inspired and values based."[53] They provide their members with freedom from "control, hierarchy, and micromanagement" while providing them with the freedom to "disrupt, speak out, and pursue one's aspirations."[54]

The results of radically collaborative organizations are remarkable. According to the *HOW Report*, a jaw-dropping 97% of radically collaborative organizations are high-performing, compared with 80% and 36% respectively for their "informed acquiescence" and "blind obedience" peers.[55] They out-compete their traditional hierarchical competitors on every financial dimension, including year-over-year growth in revenue, market share, and customer satisfaction.[56]

As a group, they consistently out-innovate the competition[57] and out-engage their workforce.[58] They are unburdened by the bureaucratic overhead of their management-bloated peers.[59] And their employees are more loyal, more willing to exert effort, and more willing to recommend their organization to others.[60] Radically collaborative organizations are the fastest-growing organizational archetype in the world, more than doubling in number between the 2012 and 2016 *HOW Reports* and currently comprising around 8% of the world's businesses.[61]

These results are a clarion call for dominator hierarchies. Radically collaborative organizations aren't just competitive—they're disruptive. Customers like their products and services better. And employees like their workplaces better. It's not a question of *if* radically collaborative organizations will disrupt your hierarchical enterprise, capturing your customers and siphoning away your employees, but when.

This book, in addition to surveying large organizations, dives into the histories, structures, and practices of several radically collaborative software organizations. From a self-managing consultancy in Mexico to a radically democratic product company in Switzerland; from an open-source-for-government consultancy in the US to a prosperity-for-all cryptocurrency spread around the globe.

In short, this book examines the practices and patterns of software organizations that utilize the power of radical collaboration to unleash individual growth and financial performance. But note: this is not a how-to book. Instead, this book is meant as an introduction to the concepts around radical collaboration.

We'll begin Chapter 1 with an introduction to the four imperatives of radical collaboration: team autonomy, managerial devolution, deficiency gratification, and candid vulnerability.

CHAPTER 1

THE FOUR IMPERATIVES OF RADICAL COLLABORATION

As we saw in the introduction to this book, the world of work is haunted by disengagement, mistrust, and meaninglessness, and it is plagued with the attendant economic consequences of low productivity, performance, and innovation. The source of this plague is widely known yet rarely addressed. Its image is softened and compartmentalized through a number of modern-day corporate euphemisms, including "bureaucracy," "Taylorism," "scientific management," and "command and control." But lurking behind all of these names is the thing itself: the dominator hierarchy, a term first introduced by world-renowned social scientist Dr. Riane Eisler in her landmark work *The Chalice and the Blade*.

Within a dominator hierarchy, people are ranked and ordered, while power and resources are distributed unequally and concentrated at the top. Through a system of domination and coercion, dominator hierarchies structurally elevate the judgements of the dominators—e.g., the bosses, managers, directors, "leaders," etc.—while structurally depriving the dominated of security, autonomy, fairness, esteem, trust, and belongingness. It is this structure that is tightly correlated to the poor social and economic outcomes endemic throughout most of the world. And it is this structure that is on the verge of being globally disrupted by an altogether new form of business known as *radical collaboration*.

As a way of working, radical collaboration leverages the passions, interests, and intrinsic motivations of the participants while grounding collaboration in the freely made commitments between peers. It has been pioneered over the past few decades by a rapidly expanding global cohort of corporations—some of which, like the appliance manufacturer Haier, the tomato processor Morning Star, and the home health-care nonprofit Buurtzorg, have come to rapidly dominate their industries.

By structuring themselves around the principle of linking rather than ranking, radically collaborative organizations favor networks of dynamic and self-managing teams. And by grounding themselves in partnership and equality, they feature a fluid approach to leadership dependent on context and granted by trust. Taken together, these facets of radical collaboration paint a striking alternative to the traditional corporate model—one that is as compelling for the individuals fortunate enough to belong to them as it is problematic for the traditional corporations unfortunate enough to compete with them.

That's because radically collaborative organizations are high performing, almost without exception, as illustrated by global research studies like the *HOW Report* and as detailed in the introduction. As a class, radically collaborative organizations achieve higher year-over-year revenue growth, capture increasingly larger swaths of market share, and enjoy higher levels of customer satisfaction than their hierarchical peers. By unburdening themselves of inertial bureaucracies and by supercharging innovation through high levels of trust and autonomy, they are rapidly disrupting practically every industry around the globe.

Traditional, hierarchical organizations can no longer rest on top-down planning or command-and-control directives. In order to survive, they must begin to understand, emulate, and adapt the business theory and practices that radically collaborative organizations are utilizing to not only meet the moment but to leapfrog ahead of it.

Of course, knowing what needs to be done is only half the challenge. A traditional organization that sets its sights on radical collaboration is still left with the question: How does a company become radically collaborative?

The answer lies in four conceptual imperatives: team autonomy, managerial devolution, deficiency gratification, and candid vulnerability. I call them imperatives because they are vital, prempetory, and essential for any business to seize on the opportunity for sustainable and substantial change offered by the disruption we are living in now. In the following chapters, we'll dive into the theory of each of these imperatives in turn, along with the illustrative practices and experiences of radically collaborative organizations.

But there's a catch: although the imperatives are rich and deep, they are also interdependent and can sometimes defy attempts at a clear delineation. A rudimentary understanding of all of the imperatives will help us gain a deeper understanding of any particular imperative. In this chapter, we'll survey all four imperatives and introduce the radically collaborative organizations and practices that will appear throughout the book.

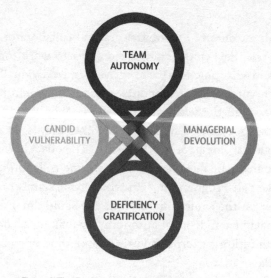

Figure 1: The Four Imperatives of Radical Collaboration

Imperative #1: Team Autonomy

Autonomy is the human need for "control over one's environment"—to feel like we "have choice within any given situation," which in turn is strongly linked to individual and organizational success.[1] As Dr. Dan Radecki, the neuroscientist and coauthor of *Psychological Safety: The Key to Happy, High-Performing People and Teams*, states: "We know from neuroscience research that people are more likely to succeed when they buy into an idea. When people reach their own insights and conclusions, solve their own problems, or come up with their own ideas . . . they are far more likely to own and implement solutions."[2]

This helps explain why radically collaborative organizations succeed where dominator hierarchies fail. Through a paradigm of domination and coercion, dominator hierarchies structurally deprive employees of autonomy, which in turn contributes to organizational woes like disengagement, mistrust, and meaninglessness.

Radically collaborative organizations, on the other hand, achieve superior levels of employee engagement and corporate innovation at least in part because they structurally gratify the need for individual and team autonomy across six core dimensions: the *how* (autonomy of practice), the *where* and *when* (autonomy of schedule), the *what* and *who* (autonomy of allocation), and the *role* (autonomy of role).

- Through **autonomy of practice**, radical collaborators control the *how* of their work. They decide how to work together as teams and what practices to collectively and individually deploy.
- Through **autonomy of schedule**, radical collaborators control the *where* and the *when* of their work. They decide whether they're collocated or distributed. Whether they sit in an office, on a couch at home, or on the beach. They decide whether to synchronize schedules to enable real-time collaboration practices like pair programming (in which two engineers program together on the same computer, at the same time) or whether to maximize individual autonomy by making asynchronous communication patterns the primary method of coordination and collaboration.
- Through **autonomy of allocation**, radical collaborators control the *what* and the *who*. Instead of being allocated to teams by a managerial hierarchy, radical collaborators self-manage allocations by freely joining teams aligned to their own interests and intrinsic motivations.
- Through **autonomy of role**, radical collaborators self-manage their own *role* within the organization. They decide what type of work they're interested in, what kind of career they want to have, and what they need from the organization in order to develop any and all necessary skills.

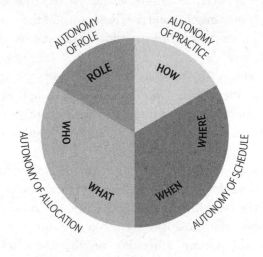

Figure 2: The Six Core Dimensions of Team Autonomy

Within this startling degree of autonomy, two clear practices have emerged among radically collaborative technology organizations. The first practice is the *outcome team paradigm*. Outcome teams are radically decoupled from specific codebases and instead focus on achieving an outcome by delivering specific units of end-user value, called *features*. In order to deliver that value, they are allowed to commit to any and all codebases they deem necessary. (See Chapter 2 for a discussion on how outcomes teams differ from feature teams).

The second practice is *human-centered design*. Radically collaborative teams don't just create products *for* users but *with* users, by getting out of the office and into the world to understand the lives and lived experiences of their users and by engaging users directly in the software making process. (We'll go further into depth on both these practices in Chapter 2.)

Imperative #2: Managerial Devolution

Radically collaborative organizations are formed and maintained through the devolution of management—i.e., through the decentralization of power out of a static dominator hierarchy and into a dynamic heterarchy of self-managing teams.

Heterarchy refers to a system of organization that is ordered yet nonhierarchical. The term first emerged in the 1970s in sociological and anthropological literature in an attempt to address social structures that are not based on a hierarchical ranking and yet clearly possess order. As the anthropologist Dr. Carole Crumley explains,

> Many structures, both biological and social, are not organized hierarchically. There is nothing intrinsically hierarchical about an oak tree or a symphony, yet each has undeniable structure and constitutes an orderly representation of the relations among elements. Nonetheless, few terms identify other kinds of order. Hierarchy—inasmuch as it is often a reductionist metaphor for order—has disproportionately influenced theory building in both social and natural scientific contexts. . . . Heterarchy may be defined as the relation of elements to one another when they are unranked, or when they possess the potential for being ranked in a number of ways.[3]

Thus, self-managing teams are based on the concepts of partnership and equality, and they are united in the belief that leadership is contextual—that it is granted by the trust of peers and limited to the situation at hand.

In fully devolved organizations, these networks of teams collectively self-manage the organization. For example, radical collaborators dynamically take on decision-making authority through devolutionary management practices like the *advice process*, *ad hoc leadership teams*, and *Holacracy®-powered governance*. (These practices are discussed in depth in Chapter 3.)

Radical collaborators also self-manage traditional managerial responsibilities like hiring, firing, and onboarding. They even self-manage the compensation process by rejecting coercive practices like performance evaluations and replacing them with devolved compensation methods like the *fractal organizational model*, the *Deming pay system*, and *self-managed pay* (discussed in depth in Chapter 3).

Imperative #3: Deficiency Gratification

As noted in Imperative #1: Team Autonomy, dominator hierarchies systematically deprive us of autonomy, but they also deprive us of a number of other psychological needs, like security, fairness, esteem, trust, and belongingness. The field of positive psychology refers to environments like this as "growth-inhibiting" structures because they structurally inhibit our personal growth and actualization by inducing a state of need-deficiency within us.[4]

Radically collaborative organizations, by contrast, are referred to as *deficiency gratifying* environments because they repeatedly and systematically gratify our higher-level human needs.[5] The radically collaborative organizations featured in this book accomplish this by combining an overall sociocultural paradigm of partnership and equality with interpersonal, deficiency-gratifying practices like *balance scores*, *Holacracy-powered check-ins*, *peer pods*, and *coin ceremonies* (all discussed in depth in Chapter 4). Thanks to this arrangement, the radical collaborators within these environments can repeatedly satisfy each other's deficiency needs for security, autonomy, fairness, esteem, trust, and belongingness.

It's important to note that this wellspring of deficiency gratification isn't just a boon for individual well-being and fulfillment; it also feeds into a foundation of collective trust, with powerful downstream consequences for organizational efficacy. For example, according to the *HOW Report*, high levels of trust lead radically collaborative organizations to exhibit thirty-two times the risk-taking, eleven times the innovation, and six times the business performance over their traditional hierarchical competitors.[6]

A number of twentieth-century psychologists, including the positive psychologist Abraham Maslow and the humanist psychologist Carl Rogers, hypothesized that the dichotomy between individual well-being and corporate profit was false.[7]

For example, in their paper "Active Listening," Carl Rogers and Richard Farson state,

> The things that are best for the individual are best for the company. This is a conviction of ours, based on our experience in psychology and education . . . . We find that putting the group first, at the expense of the individual, besides being an uncomfortable individual experience, does not unify the group. In fact, it tends to make the group less a group. The members become anxious and suspicious.[8]

Also, in *The Farther Reaches of Human Nature*, Abraham Maslow says,

> Eupsychian conditions of work are often good not only for personal fulfillment, but also for the health and prosperity of the organization, as well as for the quantity and quality of the products or services turned out by the organization. The problem of management (in any organization or society) can then be approached in a new way: how to set up social conditions in any organization so that the goals of the individual merge with the goals of the organization.[9]

Thanks to empirical studies like the *HOW Report*, we now know that these researchers were right. We don't have to choose between the well-being of individuals and the success of corporations. The former is, in fact, a multiplier of the latter.

Imperative #4: Candid Vulnerability

While dominator hierarchies are ensnared in a quagmire of defensive reasoning—in which people hide and defend their underlying assumptions and beliefs from others in an attempt to maintain unilateral control—radically collaborative organizations sparkle with openness and transparency. That's because radically collaborative organizations are sustained by a culture of *candid vulnerability*, or as it is more formally known in sociology, Model II: Productive Reasoning.

Radical collaborators candidly share their underlying thoughts, feelings, beliefs, and assumptions, thereby making their thought processes vulnerable to collective examination, critique, and even invalidation. This, in turn, feeds into an overall organizational culture of learning and collaborative innovation. By helping people separate their ideas from their egos, candid vulnerability enables the collective evolution of ideas.

The radically collaborative pioneers featured in this book have created or adopted a bevy of techniques in order to help their members cocreate a culture of candid vulnerability. From *"thinking versus saying" two-column exercises* that uncover defensive reasoning to practices like balance scores and *Holacracy-powered check-ins* for increasing psychological success (all discussed further in Chapter 5), our pioneers have created the conditions for the spontaneous emergence of candid vulnerability within their organizations at large.

The Pioneers:
Exploring the Radical Collaborators of Today

The four imperatives of radical collaboration were derived from the practices and experiences of a number of radically collaborative organizations. Some of these organizations you've already met, like the industry giants Haier, Morning Star, and Buurtzorg. Others you'll meet in the pages to come. Some had the privilege of starting with radically collaborative principles and structures. Others have gone through a process of managerial devolution and radically collaborative transformation.

Regardless of where they started, or how far they've come, their experiences cross-cut a significant range of industries and organizational sizes, forming a rich tableau for us to explore and dissect. These companies come from different industries, range in size significantly, and began their radically collaborative transformations at different points in time in their development. For your convenience, Table 1 features a list of all the organizations featured in this book, along with some key demographics and differentiating features.

These organizations have pioneered a bevy of radically collaborative practices that we'll explore throughout this book and that we'll preview in the next section.

Table 1: Radically Collaborative Pioneers

Name	Description	Demographics	Started with Radical Collaboration (RC) or Transformed?	Notable for...
Buurtzorg	Number one home health-care provider in the Netherlands.	15,000 people. Founded in 2006. Started in Netherlands, now in 25 countries.	Started with RC.	Broken up into thousands of small, self-managing teams of nurses who self-manage everything from nursing, to hiring, to customer acquisition and facilities.
CivicActions	Open-source government consultancy.	100 people. Founded in 2004.	Started with RC.	One of the first fully distributed technology companies. Notable for decentralized, grassroots-organizing culture.
cLabs/Celo	Cryptocurrency company focused on creating the conditions for prosperity in developing communities around the world.	150 people. Founded in 2018. Based in Berlin, Buenos Aires, and San Francisco.	Started with RC.	Notable for use of Holacracy.
GrantTree	Helps organizations acquire government R&D grants.	65 people. Founded in 2010. Based in London.	Transforming toward RC.	Notable for pioneering self-managed pay.
Haier	Number one appliance manufacturer in the world.	80,000 people. Founded in 1920.	Transformed to RC.	Notable for radically collaborative structure of self-managing microenterprises.
Haufe-umantis	Collaboration and talent-management software company.	200 people. Founded in 2002. Based in Switzerland.	Transforming toward RC.	Notable for transitioning from dominator hierarchy, to workplace democracy, to self-management/radical collaboration.
Matt Black Systems	Manufacturer of airplane instruments.	30 people. Founded in 1973.	Transformed to RC.	Notable for fractal organizational model.

Morning Star	Largest tomato processor in the world.	4,000 people. Founded in 1990.	Started with RC.	No managers, no set roles or responsibilities. 100% self-managing structure redesigned annually through CLOUs (colleague letters of understanding)
Nearsoft (now Encora)	"Nearshore" software consultancy.	450 people. Founded in 2006. Based in Mexico. Acquired by Encora in 2020. Currently the Mexican division of Encora.	Started with RC.	"No" rules: No bosses. No "employees." No titles. No secrets. Motto: "Freedom in the Workplace."
Pod Group	Enterprise network operator (ENO) for Internet of Things	25 people. Based in San Francisco. Founded in 1999.	Transformed to RC.	Notable for self-managing culture and self-managed pay.
TIM Group	Fintech org focused on trade advice and investment recommendations.	London-based. Acquired in 2018. 50-person self-managing group at time of acquisition.	Transformed to RC.	Notable for gradual, employee-led transformation toward radical collaboration via a management reading group.
Viisi	Fintech org focused on mortgage advice.	40 people. Based in the Netherlands. Founded in 2010.	Started with RC.	Notable for implementing the Deming pay system.
W. L. Gore	Innovation organization focused on industrial and chemical innovation	Over 11,000 employees. Founded in 1958. Based in Delaware. Revenues in excess of $3 billion.	Started with RC.	One of the first radically collaborative companies in the world. Open allocation process for teams and new innovation projects.

Radically Collaborative Practices

A radically collaborative practice is any practice that helps an organization achieve a state of radical collaboration—in which teams are autonomous, relationships are deficiency gratifying (in which people mutually satisfy each other's higher-level human needs), collective learning is enabled through candid vulnerability, and management is no longer the purview of a static dominator hierarchy but rather the shared responsibility of a dynamic heterarchy.

We are still in the early days of radical collaboration. Pioneering organizations are constantly innovating and inventing new practices and structures. Neither the list below nor the practices themselves are definitive. Therefore, think of these practices not as a blueprint but as a starter kit for radically collaborative transformation and experimentation.

Radically Collaborative Software Practices
- **Outcome team paradigm:** Outcome teams are cross-functional and aligned to the delivery of user value while being radically decoupled from codebases. In order to deliver user value, an outcome team may directly modify and deploy any and all codebases within the organization, regardless of who created them or normally maintains them.
- **Bubbles:** A process for organically generating, or "bubbling up," short-lived outcome teams centered around a particular initiative. These "bubbles" automatically dissolve, or "pop," once the initiative is complete.
- **Human-centered design:** A radically collaborative approach to designing and testing software solutions that brings users directly into the software-making process.
- **Pair programming:** A practice in which two engineers radically collaborate on programming by sharing the exact same computer at the same time and developing the software together, passing the keyboard back and forth.

Devolved Management Practices:
- **Advice process:** Anyone in the organization is allowed to make any decision, so long as the decision maker makes their thought process vulnerable to examination, critique, and invalidation by anyone who could be affected by the decision.
- **Ad hoc leadership teams:** In which anyone in the organization can announce an initiative to change something about the organization and anyone interested can join. The ad hoc team has full authority to make any change, so long as they are transparent about the process they go through.
- **Holacracy-powered governance:** A rigorously efficient process for the collective evolution of an organization's structure and roles. It enables anyone in the organization, at any time,

to raise up an organizational tension and have it immediately processed and resolved.

- **Peer pods:** Self-managed groups of peers providing ad hoc coaching, mentoring, and support for each other in their careers.
- **Onboarding buddies/"sponsors":** In which a radical collaborator sponsors an incoming colleague, pairing with them for a number of days or weeks in order to help the new colleague orient themselves within a nonhierarchical environment and to find their place within it.
- **Job fairs:** In which new and potential projects are laid out to the organization for radical collaborators to consider freely joining.

Devolved Compensation Practices

- **Deming Pay System:** In which everyone in the organization receives a predetermined, transparent salary that is then automatically incremented every year through predetermined, transparent annual raises. Profit sharing is also distributed equally among all members.
- **Fractal organizational model:** In which everyone in the organization is a virtual company of one, complete with a balance sheet and a profit-and-loss statement. Salaries are a result of the negotiated commitments people make to each other along the value stream and the individual surpluses that results.
- **Self-managed pay:** In which individuals transparently set their own salaries and determine their own raises at any time.

Deficiency-Gratifying/Candid Vulnerability Practices

- **Balance scores:** Radical collaborators start each day by sharing with each other a score between one and ten that represents how balanced they feel between work life, home life, and spiritual life. It's a tool for increasing transparency, vulnerability, and empathy while also helping participants calibrate with each other at the beginning of a collaboration.
- **Check-ins:** Radical collaborators create a sacred space at the beginning of meetings for each other to vulnerably name what is distracting them or keeping them from being fully present in the moment.

- **Two-column "thinking versus saying" exercises:** After a challenging conversation, sit down with a piece of paper and draw a line down the middle, dividing it into two columns. On the right-hand column, transcribe the conversation from memory. On the left-hand column, write down the thoughts you were having but failing to vocalize. The delta between the two typically reveals a good deal of defensive reasoning within yourself, as opposed to candid vulnerability.
- **Biggest fail of the week:** Team members take turns sharing accidents, mistakes, and outright professional or personal failures with each other. The process creates an environment of collective support and encourages personal growth by normalizing imperfection.
- **Coin ceremony:** A ceremony in which radical collaborators freely recognize each other not for their day-to-day work but for their "being"—for who they are and what they contribute to those around them and to the world.

Conclusion

Taken together, the four imperatives of radical collaboration leverage the passions, interests, and intrinsic motivations of an organization and its people, while grounding collaboration in the freely-made commitments between peers. Although it may be tempting to cherry-pick the imperatives for your organization, it's important to remember that for an organization to enjoy long-term success with radical collaboration, it must embrace all four imperatives.

For example, team autonomy would likely end in chaos or frustration without simultaneously embracing managerial devolution. Similarly, candid vulnerability will never take root in an organization that does not first establish a community of trust and safety through a paradigm of interpersonal deficiency gratification. Engagement, growth, innovation, and performance are not the result of any particular imperative but rather the complex interplay between all of the imperatives. Thus, in the following chapters, we'll dive into each conceptual imperative in turn to elucidate both the theory and practice behind it, and we'll also deepen our understanding of their interdependencies along the way.

Before moving on, take a moment to pause and reflect on the overall idea of radical collaboration with the following questions:

Questions for Reflection

» If you had to summarize radical collaboration to someone else based on this chapter alone, what would you say?

» What about radical collaboration excites you the most?

» What about radical collaboration scares you the most?

» Based on what you've seen in this chapter, what are some of the challenges you foresee in introducing radical collaboration into your workplace?

CHAPTER 2

IMPERATIVE #1: TEAM AUTONOMY

Human beings have a deep and abiding need for autonomy. We need to control our own lives and lived experiences—to manage ourselves without the interference or domination of others; to decide from moment to moment and day-to-day what commitments we make and how we will go about honoring them. According to the field of positive psychology, our need for autonomy is "basic, or biological,"[1] and underpins other inborn human needs, like dignity and self-esteem.[2] Which is why a loss of autonomy can have such serious consequences for individuals and organizations alike.

As we saw in the introduction, dominator hierarchies structurally deprive us of autonomy, which in turn contributes to organizational woes like disengagement, mistrust, and meaninglessness, along with their attendant economic consequences. But radically collaborative organizations achieve superior economic results by structurally gratifying the need for individual and team autonomy—and no organization better illustrates this point than Haier.

By creating radically collaborative swarms of autonomous, self-managing teams, called *microenterprises*, and by scaling them to encompass over eighty thousand employees, Haier has resolved the dichotomy between individual fulfillment and corporate success. They've created an organization in which "everyone can be their own CEO,"[3] as their own CEO states. They have enjoyed some truly stunning economic outcomes as a result, but before their success, a lack of autonomy nearly brought them to the brink of ruin.

From Bad to Radical

"NO URINATION or defecation in the working area."[4] This was the sign that greeted Zhang Ruimin upon his arrival at Haier, the state-run refrigerator factory that he had been assigned to manage in the early 1980s. At the time, Haier was structured as a ruthless command-and-control dominator hierarchy and was teetering on the verge of bankruptcy. The enterprise was saddled with debt, the factory itself was a mess, and the workers, having long ago been robbed of any sense of autonomy, had lost all interest or passion in their work and had become actively disengaged, as the aforementioned sign would suggest.

This dehumanizing loss of autonomy had in turn led to a production quality nightmare. A full 20% of the factory's refrigerators rolled off the assembly line defective,[5] and although workers knew where the problems were, they had neither the authority nor the desire to solve them. Decades of a dehumanizing dominator hierarchy had robbed workers of their dignity and the company of its profits.

At the time he took over, Zhang was young and inexperienced, but he had a natural talent for inspiring change. Shortly after his arrival, he lined up seventy-six of the company's new yet defective refrigerators in the middle of the factory. After inviting all of the company's employees to join him in a giant circle around the fridges, he took a sledgehammer and smashed the first refrigerator in the line to bits. He then handed the sledgehammer to the nearest worker and encouraged her to do the same.[6]

This act was, to put it mildly, shocking. According to Zhang, a single refrigerator cost two years salary for the average Chinese worker at that time.[7] Destroying a refrigerator—even a broken one—seemed unimaginable to most employees, but destroy them they did. By passing the sledgehammer from worker to worker, they took turns demolishing the defective refrigerators while symbolically demolishing the dehumanizing dominator hierarchy that had created them in the first place.

From this revolutionary start, Zhang sparked a decades-long transformation of the company away from domination and coercion and toward autonomy and radical collaboration.

As we saw in the introduction, Haier has arrived at a company structure composed of thousands of tiny, autonomous microenterprises. These microenterprises are self-organizing teams typically consisting of ten to fifteen people, each with their own purpose, product or service, and profit-and-loss statement.

Some, like various marketing and manufacturing microenterprises, are internal and exist only to sell their services to other Haier microenterprises. Others are external-facing, focused on enhancing the lives of consumers or end-users through new, innovative products and services.

Regardless of whether they are internal or external, each microenterprise is entirely self-managing. At Haier, there are no middle managers or bureaucracy, no labyrinth of procedures or soul-crushing red tape. Instead, each microenterprise sets their own goals, makes their own plans, and freely relates to each other as they please.

For example, Lu Kailen is your typical, everyday Haier employee. But thanks to the Haier culture "that puts entrepreneurship at its heart,"[8] Lu is also the cofounder of the multimillion dollar gaming laptop microenterprise known as ThundeRobot. Here's how that came about. In 2013, Lu was a recent college graduate. While in college, he had spent a fair amount of time playing video games. However, he had become frustrated with the "lack of power, uneven screen quality, and stodgy design"[9] that most commercial laptops offered gamers like himself.

After joining Haier, he was struck with an idea: What if he leveraged Haier's entrepreneurial support system to create and sell a new hard-core gaming laptop? In most corporations, the decision to invest in a new speculative business would be the call of managers. But at Haier, it's the call of the employee. As a key facilitator within Haier's laptop microenterprises explains, "In making decisions, we have to let users and entrepreneurs speak—not managers."[10]

Lu began by leveraging Haier's internal investment platform, which gives employees "access to finance, the company name, the brand, and all connections."[11] With $270,000 in seed capital, Lu banded together with other gaming enthusiasts at Haier to create a microenterprise they called ThundeRobot.[12] They began working directly with hard-core gamers to shape the product, which in turn led to a significant word-of-mouth network and subsequent community demand. Their first batch of five hundred laptops sold out in under a minute.[13] In their second offering a few weeks later, they received eighteen thousand orders in twenty-one minutes.[14]

The radical collaborators at ThundeRobot have since scaled these results into a successful, sustainable business, with $117 million in annual sales.[15] Not bad for a hardware startup. When asked about the impact this rapid success has had on him, Lu points not to his (significant) monetary rewards, but to his experience of personal growth and collective motivation. "Never in a million years did I think I could create a company like this," Lu remarks. "Since the start of ThundeRobot, I have been able to develop myself in so many ways. My previous employer would never have allowed me to do this. I share the motivation of every person in our team. Everyone is enterprising, proactive and involved."[16]

By creating a radically collaborative culture in which every worker can become an entrepreneur, Haier has unleashed a sense of passion and intrinsic motivation that is paying dividends for employees and shareholders alike. But they're not the only ones. Radically collaborative organizations across the board leverage autonomy to structure their organizations and achieve superior economic results.

The Six Core Dimensions of Autonomy

As we looked at briefly in Chapter 1, radically collaborative organizations structurally gratify the need for individual and team autonomy across six core dimensions: the *how* (autonomy of practice), the *where* and *when* (autonomy of schedule), the *what* and *who* (autonomy of allocation), and the *role* (autonomy of role).

In a moment, we'll look at each of these dimensions in turn. However, a warning is first in order. Giving teams even a single one of these dimensions of autonomy, much less all six, flies in the face of pretty much all mainstream business theory and praxis. These dimensions challenge deeply embedded cultural assumptions about the motivations and behaviors of working people. (We will examine these assumptions, and the scientific evidence against them, in Chapter 4.)

Thus, as we consider the dimensions, you may find yourself objecting to them as idealistic, utopian, even anarchistic. And although I will illustrate these dimensions through stories from radically collaborative pioneers, some of which have practiced radical collaboration successfully for decades, you may still feel an impulse to write them off as flukes or exceptions.

Please know that your reactions are natural and normal. In fact, if the book ended with this chapter, without detailing any of the other three imperatives, your objections would be well warranted. That's because the practices that we'll learn about in this chapter do not exist in isolation from the other three imperatives.

Team autonomy is necessary for radical collaboration—but it is *not* sufficient on its own. It does not address larger challenges of organizational management, like the emergence of shared constraints and policies or the creation, distribution, and evolution of responsibilities. If team autonomy isn't coupled with managerial devolution (the topics of Chapters 3 and 4), it is just as likely to lead to fragmentation and chaos as it is to innovation and success.

Although I will attempt to anticipate specific questions and concerns throughout this chapter, know that some of them won't be fully addressed until later chapters, since it is only through the fusion of all four imperatives that your objections will be fully resolved.

Autonomy of Practice:
The *How*

The most universal dimension of autonomy among our pioneers is autonomy of practice—i.e., the *how*. Radical collaborators within these companies are free to decide among themselves, both as individuals and as teams, *how* to do their work. Should developers program individually, in pairs, or in "mobs," as is increasingly the fashion today? Individuals and teams decide. Should designers validate user experiences with prototypes before developers build it out in code? Individuals and teams decide. Should product managers engage in competitive analysis and business viability studies before charting out a product roadmap? Again, individuals and teams decide.

There's no one sitting on high in these organizations telling others how to do their jobs. Colleagues within these organizations are empowered to make these choices themselves—and to be responsible to themselves and to each other for the choices they make.

Before we dive into examples, let us address what is undoubtedly a concern on the part of many readers: If individuals and teams are free to decide how to do work, does this mean that teams can choose to ignore company priorities? Security best practices? Financial regulations? The short answer is: no.

The *how* here really refers to the "craft" behind the work—the particular set of skills and practices that team members, like product managers, designers, and engineers, utilize from moment to moment and day-to-day in pursuit of common goals and shared outcomes. The work itself (like the problem the team is solving or the outcome they're attempting to achieve) as well as the constraints around the work (like financial regulations and security requirements) can and often do emerge from a process that extends well beyond the team.

That being said, radically collaborative organizations create and embrace common constraints and shared outcomes without resorting back to a dominator hierarchy by utilizing devolutionary management practices, as the following chapter will explore.

To see "autonomy of how" in action, take TIM Group, a London-based fintech organization that provides trade ideas and investment recommendations through their online platform. During the 2010s, TIM Group underwent a gradual transformation toward radical collaboration and self-management. (We'll detail the full transformation in the Chapter 3.) They organized as a self-managing network of autonomous teams, without managers or hierarchy, and they instituted a series of agreed-upon technology constraints that balanced the need for team autonomy with cross-team fluidity.

As former CTO Jeffrey Fredrick explained in his interview with me,

> Before our transformation, we had relatively fixed teams. But as we began to transform, we said, basically, we're one department. Some decisions a team makes will impact other people. The choice of practice, like whether you pair program or not, was entirely in the team. And so some teams paired daily, others would pair occasionally. But bringing in new technologies like MongoDB, or new languages like Scala, impacted everyone, especially as teams began to focus on delivering outcomes and user value irrespective of the codebases involved.

This led to the emergence of a cultural meme among the team, as former TIM Group developer Graham Allan told me. "The idea of reducing the technology surface area really became a [cultural] meme within the group. How do we simplify this? How do we keep it streamlined?"

hierarchy to workplace democracy to self-management/radical collaboration.

The theme of team autonomy through liberating constraints is also visible at Haufe-umantis, a radically collaborative software company focused on talent management and collaboration. They have implemented autonomy of practice by adapting a popular Agile methodology called Scrum to their radically collaborative organization. Although many software teams within the organization are united around a shared purpose and goal, they are individually empowered through Scrum to decide how to best go about achieving that goal.

As Sergi Rodriguez, a front-end developer at Haufe-umantis, explained in his interview with me,

> I feel like we are independent as a team because no one is going to come and say, "Hey, you have to do it this way or that way." At the same time, we have shared goals and agreed-upon guidelines. But these limitations make sense. It's not something that we feel is being forced on us. It's better for everyone to have some shared constraints—because those constraints liberate us to be autonomous and self-organizing.

A Note on Scrum

Let me pause here for a moment to address a concern about Scrum. If you have experience with Agile software development, then there's a good chance you already have experience with Scrum. Unfortunately, there's also a good chance that you've experienced a mangled, watered-down, hierarchical form of Scrum. That's because few corporate enterprises have adopted Scrum in any authentic sense.

Scrum was born out of an effort to empower cross-functional teams with autonomy and self-management on a basis of partnership and equality, as the official Scrum Guide makes plain: "Scrum Teams are cross-functional, meaning the members have all the skills necessary to create value each Sprint. They are also self-managing, meaning they internally decide who does what, when, and how."[17]

Yet, instead of empowering teams, most organizations have implemented Scrum by sprinkling a few Scrum practices on top of their hierarchical waterfall development process and calling it a day. This has given Scrum a bad reputation in many Agile circles—particularly rarefied circles like Extreme Programming. But few of those who bad-mouth Scrum have experienced an authentic Scrum organization. If they had, they would not be so quick to write Scrum off.

An authentic Scrum organization is like an organizational science lab. The organization is continuously experimenting with how it works and organizes itself. No two teams work quite the same way, and even a single team experiments with their ways of working from one month to the next. Anyone frustrated with dogmatic Agile adherents convinced that they've discovered the "One True Way" would do well to seek out an authentic Scrum organization.

Autonomy of Schedule:
The *When* and the *Where*

If deciding how to work is the most ubiquitous form of autonomy among our pioneers, then deciding when to work is the runner up. As organizations increasingly shift their focus from how people work to what they achieve, the need to control when people work becomes increasingly nonsensical.

The majority of the radically collaborative organizations featured in this book practice autonomy of schedule, in which colleagues decide when they work and where they work. There's no nine-to-five schedule, no time clocks, no office managers monitoring butts in seats or hands on keyboards. Early birds can get started before the rooster crows. Night owls can warm themselves at the glow of their terminals long after others have gone to bed. If someone wants to spend Sunday afternoon programming and Monday morning rock climbing, they're free to do so. And if someone wants to take that conference call while sunning themselves on the beach, have at it.

Before we see this process in action, let me anticipate some of the more immediate objections. If people are free to make their own schedules, how do you ensure that the necessary coordination and interactions between teammates and colleagues happen? If some teammates choose to work on Sunday evening and go rock-climbing on Monday morning, how do you know that they're not leaving the rest of their teammates in the lurch?

These objections tend to be based on an assumption that employees, if given the choice, will selfishly pursue their own interests at the expense of the organization. We'll address this assumption (known as *Theory X*) in detail in Chapter 4, but for now, I'll summarize a few basic points.

In one sense, it's accurate to say that people do indeed pursue their own interests—but rather than fight against it, as dominator hierarchies do, radically collaborative organizations embrace and leverage this fundamental aspect of human nature. By increasing the sense of control and choice that people have over their work, radically collaborative organizations increase the likelihood that their members work on projects they care for and with people they care about.

When human beings band together, not because they are forced to but because they autonomously *choose* to based on shared goals and intrinsic motivations, they are more likely to succeed (as we noted in Chapter 1), and they are also more likely to work together responsibly. A teammate who cares about their team and their team's work does not typically jeopardize their collective efforts through the capricious misuse of autonomy of schedule.

In other words, although giving people autonomy over their schedules seems like it would increase coordination and productivity challenges, the opposite is more likely. When autonomy of schedule is combined with the other dimensions of autonomy surveyed in this chapter, productivity and coordination challenges *decrease* as people become more likely to work on projects and teams that align with their own intrinsic motivations and as people gain an authentic sense of responsibility over their work.

AT A GLANCE

CivicActions: Open-source government consultancy. One hundred employees. Founded in 2004. One of the first fully distributed technology companies. Notable for decentralized, grassroots-organizing culture.

Take CivicActions, a radically distributed consulting company that focuses on creating open-source and open-data solutions for governments. Founded by two early open-source community advocates, Henry Poole and Aaron Pava, and started with an emphasis on self-organizing, distributed networks of people and teams, CivicActions has built the company from the ground up on the idea that colleagues can figure out for themselves when and where to work. There's no offices, and no nine-to-five schedule. If someone wants to sleep in everyday and start working after lunch, that's up to them. If someone wants to spread their work out throughout the day in order to better balance the needs of work and the needs of home life, then more power to them.

As Pava, cofounder of CivicActions, explained to me in our interview,

> With the exception of the couple of mandatory calls that you're expected to be on, like your team standup and the all hands, you have complete autonomy of schedule. Some stick to a nine-to-five sort of schedule; others don't. We have early birds on the East Coast who have little to no synchronous overlap with night owls on the West Coast.

This approach has helped CivicActions leverage the talents of geographically dispersed colleagues as the company has grown. It has also made it possible for them to more easily weather the COVID-19 pandemic. Their company was already *entirely* distributed before the pandemic and its subsequent lockdowns hit. And colleagues already made up their own hours.

Although some had to adjust their individual schedules to deal with the reality of quarantining with their children, the company itself never had any assumptions about when people did their work in the first place. If someone needed to work in the mornings or evenings and take care of their children during the day, they could do so without impacting the organization.

The only significant change in the culture that Pava has seen is that colleagues have begun to record most synchronous interactions for anyone who can't be there.

> We've basically created a culture of recording every single full-team call and most group calls and posting the recording afterward in the Slack channel. So if anyone, for whatever reason, wasn't able to be there, they could catch up asynchronously. Although we all want to have a world where it's like, "This could have just been an email," sometimes you really do need to hear and see the interactions to truly understand the outcomes and decisions.

Haufe-umantis, the Swiss-based radically collaborative company building talent management and team collaboration tools, has implemented autonomy of schedule as well. Their teams set out goals at the beginning of a two-week sprint, but the decision about how and when to achieve those goals is entirely up to them.

As one of their developers, Sergi Rodriguez, pointed out to me, "Teams are free to work when they want, where they want. The goal is to achieve the sprint, not work a certain number of hours at a certain time."

If developers like to spend their nights programming and days enjoying the outdoors, they're free to do so. And if they complete their sprint a week early, they're also free to spend the remaining time however they please. This is the agile equivalent of what is more broadly known today as a *ROWE*, or a results-only work environment.

In a ROWE, people are accountable not for how they work or when they work but for what they achieve, and some large organizations, like Best Buy and GAP, have begun to experiment with it. But to be clear, most ROWE workplaces in existence today are still hierarchical organizations. Accountability in these workplaces means being assigned work by a manager and being at the whim of that manager's judgements when they evaluate your results.

But our pioneers prove that a ROWE is also possible in the absence of a dominator hierarchy. As we'll see in Chapter 3, Nearsoft colleagues, for example, are accountable not to a boss but to their colleagues directly, who can band together and fire a teammate if they believe that person is intentionally and persistently shirking their duties.

Ricardo Semler, the former CEO of Semco Partners, a radically collaborative conglomerate based in Brazil, wrote an entire book about autonomy of schedule. He called it *The Seven-Day Weekend*—a metaphor for the life-affirming possibilities that autonomy of schedule can offer. Semler formed his company around the idea that people should be free to decide on their own schedules. As he wrote, "If the workweek is going to slop over into the weekend—and there's no hope of stopping that from happening—why can't the weekend, with its precious restorative moments of playtime, my time, and our time, spill over into the workweek?"[18]

During his tenure, Semco grew from "annual sales of $4 million . . . to $212 million, with 40 percent annual growth and a less than 2 percent employee turnover rate."[19] Semler believed that their success proved that "the repetition, boredom, and aggravation that too many people accept as an inherent part of working can be replaced with joy, inspiration, and freedom."[20] Most of all, he believed that when people are free to make their own schedules, they can find a balance that makes both their working lives and their personal lives more gratifying.

In this belief, Semler's not alone. The notion of balance is at the core of CivicActions as well. And as we will see in Chapter 5, that belief has led the colleagues at CivicActions to generate a variety of practices that help people find balance in their lives and that give them the safety, trust, and belongingness they need to sustain and maintain that balance.

The Four-Day Work Week

Although it's not technically a form of "autonomy of schedule," it's worth noting that the "four-day work week" movement gaining steam around the world and recently made into law in Iceland is at the very least a fellow traveler to the practices and ideas within this section. The four-day work week is both an attempt to give people a more equitable balance between work and life as well as a recognition of the fact that output isn't just a simple function of time.

A great deal of work, and knowledge work in particular, requires not just time but energy, motivation, inspiration, and creativity—most of which can't be produced at an even rate hour after hour or day after day. Our ability to passionately and creatively solve novel problems and adjust to rapidly changing business needs is at least as dependent upon our time away from work as it is dependent on our time at work—and the four-day work week is a solid attempt to recognize that reality.

Autonomy of Allocation:
The *What* and the *Who*

So far, we've looked at dimensions of autonomy that fall squarely within the sphere of self-management. When we decide when to do something and how to do something, we are self-managing our work tasks. But self-management still leaves open the possibility that the work tasks themselves are assigned by a manager. So, what if individuals controlled not only the *how* and the *when*, but the *what* and the *who*?

What would happen if instead of being assigned to projects by managers, employees chose for themselves what projects to work on and what teams to join? The idea, known as autonomy of allocation, isn't as crazy as it sounds. Within the domain of knowledge work—in which workers solve novel problems through an iterative process that combines specialized skills with ongoing discovery and learning—the self-selection of projects and tasks can be more efficient than the managerial control of allocations.

In a 2021 study of allocation methods, researchers at the University of California, the University of Venice, and the Institut Européen d'Administration des Affaires reported the following:

> We find that letting employees pick the tasks they are most skilled at is advantageous in . . . project-based organizations with strong specialization and low interdependence. . . . Two important benefits of self-selection that arise from individual level attributes are a higher level of motivation and greater alignment between skills and tasks than what would be obtained under authority-based allocation.[21]

The obvious concern that most people have when hearing about autonomy of allocation is this: If everyone gets to decide what they work on, who will do the boring, hard, or dirty work that no one else wants to do? In other words, "Sounds great—but who cleans the toilets?"

At pretty much any traditional organization, in which people are disengaged from their work, mistrustful of their leaders and coworkers, and plagued by a sense of meaninglessness in their jobs, this would be a valid concern. The likelihood that individuals will sacrifice their personal interests in pursuit of a greater good is next to nil in an organization in which no greater good exists. But in a radically collaborative organization, in which 98% of employees are authentically dedicated, 97% are deeply accountable, and 97% are fully responsible for their work and actions,[22] the likelihood for people to collectively share and shoulder the burden of inglourious work tasks significantly improves.

Case in point: take the GE/Durham jet engine factory, a radically collaborative manufacturing organization that we'll study in detail in the next chapter. At this factory, the workers self-allocate into teams and self-commit to roles on those teams based on their intrinsic motivations. But they also take responsibility for their work environment.

As Charles Fishman, the three-time winner of the Gerald Loeb Award, the most prestigious prize in business journalism, notes, "In addition to building engines, everyone serves at one time or another on one of several work councils that cut across team lines. The councils handle HR issues, supplier problems, engineering challenges, computer systems, discipline"—and yes, cleaning too.[23] "Some of the routines seem smaller, but they are no less essential. Despite the plant's almost operating-room cleanliness, there is no cleaning crew. Everyone cleans up."[24]

To see autonomy of allocation in action, let's turn our spotlight again on TIM Group. When a developer-led reading and discussion group within TIM Group learned about the theory of autonomy of allocation, as well as the practical experience of it in radically collaborative organizations like GE/Durham, they were keen to try the idea out for themselves. And when a gaggle of business owners came to them with new application and feature ideas, they decided this was just the moment to run an experiment. They called it the job fair.

Here's how it worked. The business owners took turns presenting their requests for new applications or new features in existing applications. Developers asked questions and sought clarifications but refrained from openly stating a preference. After the presentations and Q&As were over, the business owners left. The developers then discussed the projects among themselves and flagged projects they wanted to personally work on. After everyone chose their desired projects, they reassembled the business owners and presented them with the allocation results.

The subsequent results conversation could get awkward at times, since sometimes developers wouldn't sign up for some of the projects that the business owner requested. Developers turned them down for a number of reasons. For example, the project as presented might have been vague or confusing. Or the developers might have deemed it unimportant relative to their other projects or to their existing work.

A project might even have been passed over because of the business owner behind it. For example, on one occasion a developer had to inform a business owner that no one chose his project because no one likes working with him.

In other words, autonomy of allocation through job fairs not only gave developers the chance to work with people they liked and on projects that appealed to their intrinsic motivation, it also surfaced valuable feedback on the business ideas as well as the personalities behind them.

In a dominator hierarchy, poorly conceived projects and domineering personalities can simply be forced onto makers.* But autonomy of

---

*Throughout this text, we will often use the term "maker" as a shorthand for "software maker" or even more generally "knowledge worker." The term "maker" is emphasized not only because it is inclusive of many different roles—like developers, product managers, and designers—but because it emphasizes the creative aspect of knowledge work. Knowledge workers create, or *make*, knowledge products through the creative deployment of problem-solving techniques to novel challenges and opportunities.

allocation eliminates this dysfunction. When people are free to follow their intrinsic motivation, their choices shine a light on troubled projects and troubling personalities. Over time, problems like these tend to self-correct. Vague or unconvincing projects get reformulated while troubling personalities either learn how to collaborate or leave.

AT A GLANCE

cLabs: Cryptocurrency company focused on creating the conditions for prosperity in developing communities around the world. Employs 150 people. Founded in 2018. Based in Berlin, Buenos Aires, and San Francisco. Notable for its use of Holacracy.

Another take on autonomy of allocation comes from cLabs, a radically collaborative cryptocurrency company focused on giving everyone access to the conditions for property. Pranay Mohan, a software engineer at cLabs, told me about how his experience with autonomy of allocation helped him discover what it was that he was truly passionate about.

A few months into his tenure at cLabs, he pursued an opportunity to work on a proof-of-concept blockchain application for the World Bank Group, a world-renowned NGO. Although he had no prior experience working with NGOs, he felt inspired by the World Bank Group's mission and track record of results. However, after joining the effort, he discovered that he had little interest in the slow-moving realities of NGO work, which, of necessity, require one to navigate an immensity of political and bureaucratic complexities.

After spending a few months working with the World Bank Group, he returned to his former work on crypto protocols. As Mohan noted during our interview,

> From a purely economic standpoint, it's inefficient for an organization to let someone like me pursue an area of work only to drop it once I discover that it's not aligned to my own interests and sense of purpose in the world. But in the long term, it allows that self-selection process to be more efficient. By tolerating that initial inefficiency of exploration, people end up settling and finding a home and things that are much more germane and amenable to what they see themselves doing long term.

By reassuming a role focused on the core crypto technology itself, Mohan could better serve the organization. But had he never been given the chance to explore, he might not have discovered where his real passions lie.

This is the power of autonomy of allocation. By giving people the chance to find the work that truly inspires them and ignites their passion, radically collaborative organizations can leverage the power of intrinsic motivation to achieve superior economic results.

As researchers at the Legal Research Network summarized,

> Self-Governing organizations create both more freedom from control, hierarchy, and micromanagement, and more freedom to disrupt, speak out, and pursue one's aspirations. . . . They attract people who are inspired to contribute their full character and creativity in pursuit of a shared purpose, and give them the freedom to actualize their full potential. As a result, these organizations outperform by all meaningful measures.[25]

In fact, the Legal Research Network found that 94% achieved higher levels of market share, business results, and customer satisfaction as compared to their hierarchical competitors.[26]

We've now arrived at a state of autonomy in which people can choose what they work on, who they work with, when they work, where they work, and how they work. But we've still left open the possibility for managers to decide what role people play. What would happen if people were free to choose roles for themselves?

Autonomy of Role

What if you're a back-end developer who's bored with programming but has a budding passion for user research? Or what if you're a manual tester that secretly wants to get into product management?

At most organizations, you would likely have little choice but to quit your job, take out a student loan, and go back to school. But radically collaborative organizations are not like most organizations. In addition to all of the other forms of autonomy we've already seen, many of them also feature *autonomy of role*—i.e., the power to choose, for yourself, what role to play.

Before you slam the book shut in disbelief, you should know that there has been a wealth of research into the positive organizational benefits that autonomy of role provides. When people have a hand in crafting their own jobs and responsibilities, both the individual and the organization benefit. As researchers recently summarized,

> Higher job motivation and better match between individual skills and tasks have also been observed when self-selection occurs during the course of job crafting—the process through which individuals alter the task, relational, and cognitive boundaries of their jobs. Job crafters alter their tasks—whether formally or informally—thus incorporating an element of self-selection into their sphere of responsibilities. Self-selecting into crafted tasks enables job crafters to contribute to their organization in ways that their formal job does not anticipate and simultaneously enables job crafters themselves to learn new skills or apply skills they own but rarely get to exercise. As a result, job crafting has been positively linked with increased job satisfaction (a sense of personal fulfillment derived from the job), job effectiveness (a person's ability to fulfill the goals and expectations of her job), organizational commitment (a person's psychological attachment to the organization), work engagement (a positive state of mind while performing the job), and an enhanced sense of self-worth.[27]

AT A GLANCE

Nearsoft: A "nearshore" software consultancy in Mexico. 450 employees. Founded in 2006; acquired by Encora in 2020. Known for its "No" rules: No bosses. No "employees." No titles. No secrets.

To see how this works in practice, consider Nearsoft (now part of Encora)—a "nearshore"* consulting organization based in Mexico but

---

*The term *nearshore* applies to consulting agencies that provide cost-effective staff augmentation services to clients in other countries with shared timed zones. In the case of Nearsoft, the Mexico-based developers there already live in the same time zones as their US clientele. As a term, nearshore is intended to mimic yet contrast with offshore, in which consultants live and work in drastically different time zones from their clientele.

works with American clientele. At Nearsoft, no one has any formal titles or manager-provided roles. Although people are originally hired into the organization because their skill set corresponds with a project need, they are free to decide for themselves what role they would like to play within the organization and what career transitions make sense for them.

Esau Batencourt, for example, joined Nearsoft because his skills as a back-end Java developer were needed on a client project. But over time, he grew bored with Java development. Instead of building back ends for business applications, he wanted to focus on building out platforms and server infrastructure for DevOps organizations—something he'd never done professionally and yet felt motivated to pursue personally.

The organization responded by first connecting him with others already doing that type of work and then helping him find a client that wanted that kind of consulting help. As he explained to me, "It's the organization's job to help you get to where you want to be, not to tell you whether or not you can do it."

Another Nearsoft colleague, Nyx Zamora, told me that when you want to transition from one role to another, "you can either wait until a client opportunity opens up that would support the transition or you can just say, 'You know what, I just want to stop right now. I have a three-month plan to start studying this and change my role.'"

At first she found this level of autonomy frightening. "It's a big decision to make. But the founders remind us, 'We hired you because you're a responsible adult. You can do what you want.'"

At Nearsoft, colleagues are trusted to exercise their autonomy responsibly and to learn from any mistakes that they make along the way.

Another take on autonomy of role comes from cLabs, the radically collaborative cryptocurrency company we met earlier in this chapter. cLabs chose to seed their organization with a ready-made framework for radical collaboration known as *Holacracy*.

If you've never heard of Holacracy, you can basically think of it as a radically collaborative starter kit for organizations, providing them with an opinionated set of rigorously defined rules for how to structure and collectively govern radical collaboration, all of which is spelled out in the Holacracy constitution.[28]

These rules enable colleagues to get work done. But they also enable them to set aside personal agendas and egos so that they may collectively evolve the organization's roles and structures.

As Holacracy's founder Brian Robertson notes,

> Holacracy's systems and processes are about continually helping the organization find its own unique identity and structure to do its work in the world, while protecting it from human agendas, egos, and politics. Holacracy allows the organization to be more driven by its own unique purpose in life, like a child developing its own identity and goals beyond those of its parents.[29]

Within a Holacracy, roles consist of a purpose, a set of domains or properties that the role has exclusive authority to control, as well as a set of accountabilities that explicitly state what the role does. For example, a marketing role might be given the following purpose: "Increase positive buzz about the company."

To achieve this, its domains might include the company's mailing lists and social media accounts. And its accountabilities might include "promoting and highlighting the organization's services to potential customers via the mailing list and social media channels."[30]

Anyone in the organization that accepts the marketing role would be duty-bound to fulfill the purpose, steward the domains, and honor the accountabilities spelled out in the role's definition. But here's where it gets interesting: no one in the organization can be forced to accept a role by anyone else. In a Holacracy, individuals are responsible for accepting, rejecting, or resigning roles. And although a specific Holacracy-powered role, called the lead link, is responsible for aligning roles to people, they don't have the power to force someone to accept a role.

In practice, this means that people pursue roles that they are actually motivated to take, regardless of whether or not they are qualified for that role on paper.

As Brian Robertson explains,

> Because Holacracy is all about organizing the work, not the people, it leaves quite a bit of freedom for the people to self-organize around what roles they fill. Instead of getting organized as single nodes in the corporate hierarchy, people are left to act more like free agents, able to shop around and accept role assignments anywhere in the organizational structure, including filling several roles in many different parts of the organization at once.[31]

Cross-Team Organizational Practices

Across the six core dimensions of autonomy—the how, when, what, where, who, and role—you might be led to assume that few, if any, cross-team organizational practices would emerge among our pioneers. But you would be wrong. Two particular trends feature predominantly in radically collaborative technology organizations: the *outcome team paradigm* and *human-centered design*. Let's look at each of these practices in turn.

Outcome Team Paradigm

Earlier in this chapter, we saw how the developer-led reading club at TIM Group inspired a transition to autonomy of allocation after learning about the practice at radically collaborative organizations. But their readings also inspired another organizational paradigm shift, thanks to their research into GE/Durham, the radically collaborative jet engine factory we met briefly earlier in this chapter.

Unlike a traditional factory, this particular GE/Durham factory had no assembly lines. Instead, the factory workers practiced something called *group assembly*. They divided themselves into multiple autonomous groups, or teams, each containing a mix of different skills. Each team would then assemble an entire jet engine together, from start to finish, with each person on the team pitching in throughout.

In a normal assembly line, each worker would be tightly coupled to one specific skill and task. But under group assembly, workers mastered an increasingly broad range of skills as they learned how to build entire engines from scratch. This not only created a highly skilled workforce, it also created a highly resilient organization. As one employee put it, "Multiskilling is how the place is kept together. You don't hoard your skills. That way, when I'm on vacation, the low-pressure turbine can still be built without me."[32]

Although ditching assembly lines might seem like a great way to slow down production, the opposite has proved true at GE/Durham. For instance, when the factory won a bid to build a type of jet engine they had never produced before—an engine that involves learning how to put together over ten thousand parts, where "even a nut that weighs less than an ounce must be installed to a very specific tightness"[33]—a single group assembly team turned out their first engine in less than nine weeks, a timeline unheard of at GE.[34] What's more, within eight more weeks, they had figured out how to produce the engines at "13% less cost" than a neighboring GE factory that had been producing that same engine for years.[35]

Although speed and cost are two important considerations for the manufacturer of jet engines, quality matters most of all. As Charles Fishman notes, "A bad jet engine could destroy hundreds of lives."[36] In this respect, the group assembly process did not disappoint. After implementing group assembly, the defect rate fell a staggering 75%.[37]

According to Fishman, "The 170-plus people who work at this plant try to make perfect jet engines. And they come close. On average, one-quarter of the engines that GE/Durham sends to Boeing have just a single defect something cosmetic, such as a cable not lined up right or a scratch on a fan case. The other three-quarters are, in fact, perfect."[38]

In a highly competitive industry like jet-engine manufacturing, quality like this matters. Thanks to this stunning level of quality, Boeing chose to ditch engines produced by GE's competitors and single-source the "GE90" engine to power its 777 jumbo jet line—an engine made exclusively at the GE/Durham factory.[39]

Inspired by this "group assembly" ethos, the developers at TIM Group moved away from specialized teams owning specific codebases and toward cross-functional teams focused on creating end-value for users regardless of what codebases they would have to edit in the process.

As TIM Group CTO Jeffrey Fredrick explained during our interview,

Before our transformation, there were multiple teams, each owning and tightly coupled to different codebases. But this didn't enable rapid innovation. So instead of aligning teams to codebases, we aligned teams to outcomes. As a department, we'd say, "We're going to work on achieving this outcome." Then a new team would self-organize around that outcome and make any changes necessary to any codebase. This enabled us to rapidly respond to an influx of new innovation and product ideas from our business partners. Instead of static teams organized around disparate components, we could organize ourselves differently based on what the project needs were. So different teams would behave differently. They would have different practices and different skill sets related to the work to be done and the outcome to achieve.

The names for these two opposing ways of organizing software development are formally known as the *component team* and *outcome team* paradigms, and they are analogous to the assembly line and group assembly manufacturing paradigms, respectively.

The component team and outcome team paradigms were first introduced by Craig Larman and Bas Vodde in their two-volume opus *Scaling Lean and Agile: Thinking and Organizational Tools for Large-Scale Scrum*. Let's explore these terms now.

If you have ever developed software inside a traditional enterprise organization, then you have undoubtedly experienced the component team paradigm. That's because traditional enterprises, almost without exception, break up their software into dozens or even hundreds of small components, like libraries or services, and then assign specific teams to own specific components.

Under this model, when a new feature needs to be built, project managers must first figure out all of the teams that will need to modify their codebases. They must then schedule all the work, being careful to order the work in a way that satisfies the dependencies between the various components. And then, once all those changes are made, they must schedule testing teams to assemble all of the changes together and ensure that the feature works.

This process, the component team paradigm, is at the root of some of the most expensive failures in modern history.

The wonderful book *Software Runaways* by Robert Glass illustrates just how disastrous the component team paradigm can be. For example, in the 1980s, the US government contracted IBM to build air traffic control software. IBM planned out the work up front. They divided the work into components and assigned components to teams. They mapped out dependencies and created elaborate schedules, roadmaps, and Gantt charts. It looked great on paper.[40]

In practice, it was a billion-dollar debacle. The actual work revealed all manner of flaws in the planning. The software developers ran into hundreds of unforeseen problems. Each problem forced replanning and renegotiation of features and hand-offs between teams. Since hundreds and eventually thousands of developers were involved in the process, divided by components, the communication overhead reached unfathomable heights. Budget overruns and missed deadlines became the norm.[41]

This went on for an entire decade until the US government gave up on the project and pulled funding. Nowhere during the entire ten years that this charade lasted did anyone put a single piece of working software in front of an air traffic controller. As Larman and Vodde lamented in their own work, "It is extraordinary the amount of delay, overhead, unnecessary management, handoff, bad code, duplication, and coordination complexity that is introduced in large groups who organize into component teams."[42]

So what's the alternative? Outcome teams.*

The outcome team paradigm is, in essence, the group assembly model we've already seen at work in the radically collaborative jet engine factory but translated into software development. An outcome team is a team of generalists who either know, or are willing to learn, a little bit of everything. Their unit of work is the *feature*—i.e., a unit of value for the user. To implement the feature, the outcome team is allowed to directly update any piece of code their organization owns.

The outcome team paradigm has several radical consequences for an organization, beginning with code ownership. Under the component team paradigm, teams own code. They control access to their component; other teams are barred from editing it directly. But the outcome team paradigm communalizes code. Anyone and everyone can add, edit, delete, and deploy code. It does not matter what code it is, what component it belongs to, or which team created it.

This autonomy to work across the entire software stack eliminates the coordination complexity caused by the component team paradigm. As we have seen, component teams need significant upfront planning and coordination. This, in turn, discourages learning, since discoveries during the build phase wreak havoc with that upfront plan.

But under the outcome team paradigm, all that coordination disappears. Instead of planning and coordination, the emphasis becomes one of learning. To implement a feature, the team may have to learn about code and systems they have never encountered before. Although daunting at first, over time programmers become multiskilled, just like the jet engine factory workers under group assembly.

---

* The "outcome team" paradigm was originally referred to as the "feature team." But this term has since become pejorative within the software community, describing a team that has become a "feature factory," pumping out feature after feature as requested by business stakeholders without ever stopping to ask if that feature is actually creating any real value. Since that type of team is a far cry from the original intended usage, I've renamed the original "feature team" paradigm to "outcome team" paradigm to more clearly reflect the original intent. In my usage, outcome teams chase outcomes and measure success based on whether or not they have achieved that outcome, as opposed to whether or not they simply delivered a feature that was requested, irrespective of its actual value.

This broadening of skill sets allows software makers, like the jet-engine technicians, to carry on with their work regardless of who is away on vacation or who is leaving the organization. Since no one is a knowledge silo, progress toward an outcome does not depend on any specific person. As Larman and Vodde summarize, outcome team advantages include "increased value throughput, increased learning, simplified planning, reduced waste of handoff, better code/design quality, and better motivation."[43]

Our pioneer cLabs illustrates the reduction in planning and coordination that comes from autonomous, cross-functional teams. In addition to long-lived outcome teams at the engineering level, cLabs has also begun to use the Holacracy-powered governance process to create short-lived outcome teams that they call *bubbles*.

This idea first developed when cLabs ran a competition among the broader Celo open-source community to develop transaction validators for the cryptocurrencies. Running the competition required the cross-organizational collaboration between engineering, product, and marketing, all of whom had their own workloads and priorities that they were already managing.

Instead of assigning a project manager to split up and manage all the work among the different departments, they developed a temporary cross-functional team with dedicated roles from each department in order to empower a single team to effectively and autonomously own the entire competition. Once the competition ended, they disbanded the team.

In the process, however, they realized that the ability for the organization to easily self-organize short-lived, cross-organizational teams was incredibly valuable. Instead of siloed departments with competing priorities, they could create dynamic cross-organizational teams to get work done for as long as that work was needed.

They refined their governance process for quickly generating and empowering autonomy in cross-organizational teams called *bubbles*, since, like bubbles, they organically bubble up into existence and then pop when they've run their course. cLabs has since baked bubbles directly into their organization-wide sprint-planning process so they can generate bubbles as soon as they sense the need for them.

Outcome teams, like those at TIM Group, and bubbles, like those at cLabs, illustrate another important consequence of the outcome-team paradigm. By organizing work into cross-functional teams that autonomously deliver user value, everyone's focus in the organization is shifted away from internal problems and issues and toward the humans the organization exists to serve.

The discussion on a software outcome team, for example, goes from "What features are good for our component?" to "What components do we need to deliver this value for our end user?" This shift leads teams to align their priorities with the purpose of the organization. It also helps explain the other predominant trend among our radically collaborative organizations: human-centered design, the topic we turn to now.

Human-Centered Design

In a hierarchical enterprise, building software tends to involve a tremendous amount of planning, coordination, budgeting, and technical implementation but it rarely involves the user. Not so at radically collaborative software organizations. That's because they embrace a discipline known as human-centered design—a practice that builds empathy between makers and users and that not only delivers software *to* users but actually involves users directly in the software-making process.

cLabs, for example, has conducted extensive user research in Africa and Argentina, working directly with consumers and merchants to codevelop the Celo monetary system. cLabs' field work with developing communities has helped them enhance the usability and viability of their cryptocurrency platform and products, including Velora, a cryptocurrency wallet application.

If you're not familiar with cryptocurrency wallets, you can think of them as your own personal minibank, where you can save, send, and receive money. Although a number of such wallets exist, most of them are *custodial*, meaning that the keys people use to access their wallets are stored in centralized locations.

Part of what makes Velora different is that it is noncustodial, meaning people are responsible for saving and remembering the private keys they need in order to open their wallet. This is by design; cLabs is attempting to create a monetary system that can't be controlled by individual governments. Using a centralized key store would have made it easier for corrupt governments and authoritarian regimes to manipulate, block, or even control their citizens's access to their own crypto-wallets. By making the wallet noncustodial, cLabs increases the power for individuals and communities to leverage the economic potential of an independent monetary system.

But noncustodial wallets also introduce a risk. If an individual loses their key, they lose access to their wallet, along with any cryptocurrency inside of it, forever. This proved to be a key barrier to adoption, as a number of users are, not surprisingly, concerned about the irreversible loss of money.

In order to address this adoption barrier, cLabs involved users directly in the software process through human-centered design. They wound up with a solution that reduced the risk of wallet-loss without increasing the risk of government control. As Vanessa Slavich, a partner at cLabs, explained to me,

> While doing human-centered design in a refugee camp in Tanzania, we learned about the concept of saving circles. A group of people pool their money together and can then take out loans from their shared savings.
>
> For example, everyone in a circle might contribute a hundred dollars. Later a member could take out a loan of a thousand dollars to put a new roof on their house. But how do they get the money out? That's the really interesting thing. After they put the money in a special safe, they distribute the keys between different members. In order to actually open the safe, you need three keys. A single key isn't enough.
>
> This gave us an idea. What if we used a similar approach for Velora? Instead of being the sole custodian of your private key, what if you distributed portions of your key to different friends for safe keeping? That way if you forgot your key, you could still reassemble it by collecting the key pieces from your friends. That's built into our app now. You can share parts of your private key to a trusted network. This has significantly reduced wallet loss and significantly increased adoption.

CivicActions also applies human-centered design to their government consulting work. For example, they used human-centered design to help veterans struggling with PTSD and suicidal thoughts. Although the Veterans Affairs administration had resources and programs to help struggling veterans, few veterans were able to discover those resources within the VA's poorly designed systems.

After working with those veterans to redesign the VA's websites and content, CivicActions was able to put information about PTSD and suicide prevention in places that veterans would actually find them. As Andy Hawks, one of the CivicActions engineers working on this effort, explained to me, this redesign resulted in a significant drop in suicide rates among veterans, another visceral display of the power of human-centered design.[44]

Stories like these illustrate the natural synergy between radical collaboration and human-centered design. As we've seen, radical collaborators work together on the basis of partnership and equality. The six dimensions of autonomy within their organizations supercharge intrinsic motivation while honoring everyone's right as equal citizens to freely make commitments to each other and to freely honor those commitments.

Human-centered design is simply a natural extension of radical collaboration beyond the boundaries of the organization, to encompass the users the organization creates software for. By working directly with users on that same basis of partnership and equality, these technology organizations create solutions that both reflect and enhance the lives of the humans they are intended for.

Conclusion

Radically collaborative organizations are radically autonomous. Collaborators within these organizations decide how to work, when to work, and where to work. They decide what they work on, who they work with, and even what role they play. Although many fear that this degree of autonomy will lead to chaos and fragmentation, clear trends have emerged within our pioneers that prove otherwise, like the outcome-team paradigm and human-centered design.

As we'll see in the next chapter, hand in hand with autonomy is the *devolution of management*. As organizations increase individual and team autonomy, managerial responsibilities and powers devolve from a static dominator hierarchy into a dynamic heterarchy—a self-organizing network of autonomous individuals and teams.

Questions for Reflection

» What does autonomy mean to you?
» What's a time in your life when you've experienced an empowering sense of autonomy? What about a time when your autonomy was severely restricted?

» Does your organization practice any of the six dimensions of autonomy: the how, what, where, when, who, or role?

» Which dimension of autonomy would be the easiest to introduce within your organization? Which would be the hardest—and why?

CHAPTER 3

IMPERATIVE #2: MANAGERIAL DEVOLUTION

Managerial devolution is an admittedly odd-sounding phrase. (When I first mentioned the term to a friend, he said that it conjured up images of proto-humanoid managers dressed in suits and ties shrieking at employees.) Despite the colloquial connotations, *devolution* is actually a technical term for the decentralization of power. When managerial powers—like the power to hire, fire, set pay, determine priorities, or change the organization's policies and structures—are dispersed out of the hands of managers and into the organization at large, we refer to this process as *managerial devolution*. And when an organization carries this process to its logical conclusion, eliminating all of the coercive vestiges of a static dominator hierarchy, we refer to this organization as *fully devolved*.

From Managers to Self-Management

The history of TIM Group, the London-based fintech organization that we met in the last chapter, is a case study in managerial devolution. In late 2011, TIM Group was structured as a traditional corporate hierarchy. The developers were divided into software teams, each owning specific codebases and each run by a line manager. It all "worked," but no one was particularly happy with it.

When their CTO, Jeffrey Fredrick—an experienced agile practitioner and an admitted hierarchy skeptic—suggested they start a management discussion group, they were all ears. The group, open to all regardless of role, set out to learn about new ways to manage and structure organizations. Each month, they would choose an article or paper to read. Then they would get together for an hour or two to discuss it. Despite the seemingly benign set up, this discussion group eventually brought about a radical transformation within the company.

The study group began by reading about Johnsonville Sausage. This family-owned sausage maker in the American Midwest was originally structured as a dominator hierarchy and beset with workplace accidents and injuries and customer complaints. But after transitioning to a self-managing structure—in which workers set their own schedules, purchased their own equipment, and even did their own hiring and firing—they saw accidents fall, quality rise, and profits grow.[1]

The developers at TIM Group were impressed but skeptical. "It sounds amazing," went the general sentiment, "but their job is too simple. We make software, not sausage." So the study group turned to the radically collaborative GE jet engine factory that was mentioned in the previous chapter, after someone pointed out that making a jet engine is basically rocket science.

Although most GE factories exhibited the typical dominator hierarchy that you would expect to find, this particular factory was a radical outlier. At this factory, there were no assembly lines, no time clocks, and no set schedules. The workers self-organized into nine different teams, and each team built whole jet engines together, from beginning to end, with team members deciding for themselves what jobs they wanted to do and when they wanted to do them. Salaries were open and automatic, based on a technician's certification level. And the teams handled all kinds of responsibilities that were normally granted only to specialized departments—like budgeting, hiring, and firing.

The results from this factory speak for themselves. A full 75% of the engines that rolled off the assembly line were literally perfect, without even a single blemish, while the remaining 25% had only a single cosmetic defect—like a harmless scratch or smudge on a fan case. No other engine manufacturer in the world has come close to this level of quality.[2]

If radically collaborative self-management could work for something as complicated as jet engines, could it work for software development? The idea seemed harder to dismiss, and the discussions at TIM Group became more animated. However, most of the developers remained skeptical.

A jet engine, at the end of the day, is fully specified before it is built. Even if assembling and testing the ten thousand parts that go into it requires scientific precision, it still bore little resemblance to building software. Software is just too messy, too open ended, too creative to take its cues from factory work. The developers needed to see self-management at work in a knowledge organization—one that thrived on innovation and creativity, one whose work was inherently messy, open ended, and full of uncertainty.

They found it in an unexpected place: in the raincoats that kept them dry in the notoriously rainy London weather.

If you have ever purchased a raincoat, then there is a good chance you have heard of Gore-Tex, the fabric that hundreds of clothing manufacturers use to waterproof their apparel. Or, if you happen to play guitar, then you will undoubtedly be familiar with Elixir guitar strings, famous for their nanoweb coating. And you likely have a pack or two of Glide dental floss stuffed away in a drawer somewhere after promising your dentist that yes you *will* floss your teeth every night before going to bed. What you may not have realized is that the organization behind all of these products, W. L. Gore, is one of the longest-running experiments in radical collaboration and self-management of the modern era.

AT A GLANCE

W. L. Gore: Innovation organization focused on industrial and chemical innovation. Founded in 1958. Based in Delaware. Over eleven thousand employees. Revenues in excess of $3 billion. One of the first radically collaborative companies in the world. Open allocation process for teams and new innovation projects.

Founded in the 1950s by a chemical engineer frustrated with hierarchy and bureaucracy, W. L. Gore strives to be a workplace where anyone can freely collaborate. Associates at W. L. Gore self-organize into small research teams based on interest and intrinsic motivation. They make and keep their own personal commitments to each other, instead of being assigned work by a boss or pigeon-holed by explicit roles and titles. And they consult with people outside their team whenever they want to make a decision "below the waterline"—a metaphor for a decision that could inadvertently hurt the whole company, in much the same way that a mistake "below the waterline" could sink a boat.

This self-managing, radically collaborative culture has enabled the years-long, open-ended research that has resulted in technologies like Gore-Tex, Elixir Strings, and Glide dental floss. It has propelled the company from a handful of people working out of the founder's basement, to an eleven-thousand-person-strong innovation organization spread around the globe.

W. L. Gore is living proof that the practices of radical collaboration and self-management are not only possible within the context of knowledge work but invaluable. After reading papers about the inner workings of

W. L. Gore, the conversation at TIM Group shifted from "it could never work here" to "where do we start?" And when the developers looked at their own organization from this new perspective, one specific focal point emerged: line managers.

Before their transformation, development teams at TIM Group were run by a line manager. Each line manager had three distinct domains of authority over their team: They managed the performance of each individual on their team. They managed the daily work of their team. And they managed the technical direction and architecture of their team. In short, the line managers were team managers, engineering managers, and performance managers all rolled into one.

After reading about radically collaborative organizations, this concentration of power stood out like a sore thumb. As Jeffrey Fredrick told me, "We looked at the role and said, 'This just doesn't make any sense. It's all bound up together. How could we decompose it?'"

Although they didn't know it at the time, they were beginning a *devolutionary* process that would lead them to radically collaborative self-management.

They began by devolving simple responsibilities into the team itself. For example, instead of having the line manager coordinate and approve holiday schedules, they distributed that authority throughout teams and individuals. It would be up to individuals themselves to decide when to take holidays and how long to take them. It was also up to individuals to decide how to take their holiday responsibly—to coordinate with their teammates to ensure that no one would not be unnecessarily impacted by their absence. Individuals and teams happily took over this authority and quickly proved that they had no trouble managing it effectively.

Baby steps like this gave the development wing of TIM Group the confidence to take larger steps toward self-management. Next they decoupled people management from line management. Line managers were no longer responsible for the performance of the individuals on their team. Instead, developers would report to a people manager outside of their team who checked in with them through one-on-ones and conducted an annual performance evaluation.

After trying this new arrangement for a while, the developers at TIM Group began to ask, "Does this people manager role really need to exist at all? Or could we handle that role's responsibilities ourselves?"

With Fredrick's encouragement, they disbanded the people manager role entirely. To do so, they had to devolve the people manager's authority into all of the individuals themselves. People managers had been responsible for annual performance evaluations and for ongoing mentorship and support. Let's take a look at how they self-managed support and mentorship by developing a practice they came to call *peer pods*.

Instead of relying on an appointed manager for mentorship and support, the developers at TIM Group began to rely on each other. They voluntarily banded together into groups of five, taking care to ensure a good mix of people from different teams in the pod. They would meet once a week, typically for an hour—and what they did during that time was entirely up to them.

One developer, Fatema Damani, notes that her pod used the time for interpersonal support. They would take turns reflecting on their feelings, discussing their respective challenges, and getting feedback from others who, unlike a manager, "do not have a vested interest in the status quo. . . . The pod is a closed circle of unbiased people who can simply listen to how you feel and give you feedback without forming any sort of judgement."[3]

They took turns mentoring others and being mentored by others, and they took satisfaction in developing creative solutions to each other's problems. Devolving people management into the organization as a whole strengthened and spread positive dimensions of people management, like mentorship and support, while separating negative dimensions, like performance evaluations.*

If you find yourself asking, "Support networks sound great, but what about people who don't fit into self-managing cultures? People who are too controlling or too authoritarian or who are too prone to take advantage of others?" please read on. Later sections in this chapter address both the need to onboard people specifically into radical collaboration as well as how self-managing organizations fire people who, despite all best efforts, won't fit into a self-managing organization.

By unraveling the concentrated power of line managers through small, measured steps, TIM Group was able to develop a thriving culture of self-management. But I want to underscore how they began: with open-ended learning. Their transformation was inspired by the ideas they learned about in their management study group. They devolved managerial powers out of a static dominator hierarchy and into a self-managing

---

* We'll revisit peer pods in Chapter 5, "Deficiency Gratification," where we'll see that they are an example of a *deficiency gratifying* social structure.

heterarchy not because they were told to but because they themselves wanted to. Any reader interested in effecting a radically collaborative transformation would do well to follow in their footsteps.

As Peter Senge, author of the bestselling work on learning organizations *The Fifth Discipline*, famously said, "People don't resist change. They resist being changed."[4] Instead of telling or forcing people to change, let the ideas spread until they take on a life of their own.

Quite a few people who hear about managerial devolution reject it out hand, since they assume that it must lead to consensus-based decision making. If bosses are no longer allowed to call the shots, they reason, then everyone must agree on everything before anything can happen.

If that were true, then I think they would be right to reject devolution. Consensus-based decision making, although sometimes effective in very small groups, is a disaster for larger ones. The idea that everyone must agree on everything is simply not practical. There will always be disagreements, and giving everyone arbitrary veto power over any decision will lead to nothing but gridlock.

However, there's no reason that devolution must lead to consensus. None of the pioneers featured in this book practice consensus except organically, among very small groups. At a larger scale, they've developed mechanisms for decision-making and organizational evolution that do not require consensus.

From short-lived, ad hoc leadership teams at Nearsoft to the advice process at Haufe-umantis to Holacracy-powered governance at cLabs, the radically collaborative pioneers featured in this book are trailblazers of decision-making practices that enhance the spirit of collaboration within their organizations while avoiding the gridlock of consensus.

Fractal Organization as a Devolutionary Model

Matt Black Systems, a thirty-person manufacturing organization in the United Kingdom, is, so far as I'm aware, the most highly devolved business on the planet. Like several other pioneers in this book, they were once structured as a command-and-control dominator hierarchy, teetering on the verge of bankruptcy. Instead of throwing in the towel, they doubled down and, over the course of a decade, iteratively pioneered a unique model for distributing power and authority throughout their workforce.

Matt Black Systems: Manufacturer of airplane instruments. Thirty employees. Based in the UK. Founded in 1973. Notable for fractal organizational model.

I won't recount all of the details of their decades-long devolutionary journey—you can read all about it yourself in the book *500%: How Two Pioneers Transformed Productivity* by Andrew Holm, Julian Wilson, and Peter Thomson. Instead, I'll just give you a basic sketch of the organizational challenge they set out to solve and the unique devolutionary model that they landed on, called the *fractal organization*.

Matt Black Systems designs and manufactures airplane instruments—like the instruments you see in a cockpit. Airplane manufacturers contract with them to build, for example, an airspeed indicator. They give Matt Black Systems a general sketch of how they want it to look and how much space it will have within the array of instruments in the cockpit. Matt Black Systems takes those specifications and then designs and manufactures the instrument, producing as many copies of it as their customer contract calls for.

Under their old system, this work was managed by managers and supported by administrators. Managers were responsible for securing contracts, designing products, and assigning work tasks. Administrators were responsible for securing parts, handling invoices, paying taxes, and taking care of all of the regulatory requirements. The manufacturing itself was handled by the workers, who took their marching orders from their managers and were beholden to the company's administrators.

This model worked at first, but over the decades, productivity and morale declined while the ratio of managers and administrators to workers grew. Deadlines slipped, defects rose, and angry customers ballooned. Eventually, Matt Black Systems struggled to break a profit.

The owners initially brought in consultants to transform their work methods with the latest and greatest processes, like Lean Manufacturing. But despite their repeated attempts to transform their organization, they failed to achieve any significant or long-lasting change. That's when the owners tossed out the consultants, discarded all of the existing "methods," and, over the course of several years and dozens of experiments, pioneered an all-new approach to organizational self-management.

From eliminating hourly pay to tearing down the walls of their centralized parts store and eliminating entire departments, Matt Black Systems slowly and methodically devolved managerial and administrative duties throughout the organization.

By the time the dust had settled on their new model, there were no longer any managers or administrators within the company. Management, HR, accounting, finance, purchasing, inventory—one by one, they *all* disappeared, their responsibilities having been devolved into the organization.

Aside from the two owners—who no longer even stepped foot inside the factory—the only people left in the company were the workers themselves. These workers, in addition to actually designing and manufacturing products for customers, also solicited and secured contracts, purchased parts, organized work tasks, paid invoices, charged customers, managed taxes and accounting, and satisfied all of the various regulatory requirements that an aerospace instruments supplier is beholden to. In other words, the company had devolved 100% of the managerial and administrative duties from a static dominator hierarchy into a dynamic, self-organizing heterarchy.

At the heart of this new way of working is something the owners call the fractal organizational model—in which each employee is an individual version, or fractal, of the company as a whole.

Here's how the fractal model works. At Matt Black Systems, each colleague is a virtual company of one. They each own a personal profit-and-loss (P&L) account—making clear how much value they create (gross revenue), how much they spend (expenses), and the difference between the two (profit or loss). For example, a worker may purchase parts from suppliers, who could be either internal or external, use machines to turn those parts into a product, and then sell that product to a customer (again, either internal or external). Their P&L makes clear, among other things, the value they create as well as the expenses they incur—like the consumption of capital assets (e.g., machinery).

In addition to a P&L, they are also personally responsible for obeying the laws and regulations that govern their work, as if they truly were their own one-person company. That means everything from taxes to loan payments to purchasing to paper-trail requirements in case of an audit!

Matt Black Systems devolved administration through the creation of simple yet auditable instruction sets the founders refer to as *recipes*, which break down the basic administrative requirements any single individual would have were they truly their own one-person business. Here's how the owners described the devolution of administration and its benefits:

> Distilling the complexity of the entire model to the level of a single individual . . . condensed all the requirements to their simplest form . . . . Constraining the admin and management around an individual allowed costs to vary depending upon the work undertaken. Simple work required little admin, while complex projects required more . . . . By contrast, the traditional approach divides admin and management into many specialties, capable of addressing the most complex jobs. For less complex work, this cost burden outweighs the benefits of division of labor.[5]

The recipes were auditable, and by employing an independent auditor to conduct "gateway reviews" of the administrative tasks, they found that conformance to the administrative and fiduciary duties incumbent upon a manufacturing organization "consistently exceeded the level previously achieved by the centralized [administration] functions."[6] And as a bonus, "costs were also significantly lower," and "the admin Recipes entered a cycle of continuous improvement . . . driven by the problems identified at the gateway reviews. Costs continuously reduced and compliance continuously improved."[7]

I know what you must be thinking. How do the workers get anything done while also dealing with all of the administration behind it? It seems like this way of working must be a tremendous drain on productivity.

Although administrative and managerial duties are in fact extensive when aggregated across a whole organization, they are manageable when devolved to an individual. If they weren't, we would be hard-pressed to explain the millions of one-person companies in existence today. Furthermore, as counterintuitive as it sounds, by devolving all administrative responsibilities and managerial authorities, the company experienced a 500% increase in productivity. This is a feat with few, if any, parallels in the manufacturing world, so let's pause to consider what could account for it.

To begin with, the new model inspired individual entrepreneurship by maximizing the sense of ownership everyone felt over their work. Under their old command-and-control model, they felt no sense of ownership. And quite rightly, because that system denied them that sense. They were, for example, told what to do by managers, by what date, and then paid for their time. The more hours they worked, the more they got paid. If they worked overtime, their pay rate increased, leading to a perverse incentive: they were rewarded for being minimally productive.

But under the new model, each individual's pay—i.e., each virtual company's *profit*—was a function of their productivity. The more efficiently they worked, the more value they generated—and the more money they made.

This changed their entire perspective on their work. They were the owners of their work—the decisions they made directly impacted their individual bottom line. They had a vested interest in quality and productivity, and in ensuring that anyone they collaborated with or depended on also had that same vested interest. Their individual success now depended on their overall, collective success in a very direct and tangible sense.

In addition to increasing individual ownership, the new model also increased individual stewardship. Under the old model, they had no reason to be the stewards of their environment. They didn't care if machines were new or old, cheap or expensive. They didn't care if they dropped parts during work and left them scattered about the floor to waste. They didn't care if the company took out loans with unfavorable terms.

Under the new system, they themselves were directly, financially responsible for the company. Machinery, rent, loan terms—they all impacted the company's bottom line, which workers now had a stake in because each virtual company of one shouldered their portion of the whole company's financial burdens. Those burdens were reflected in their individual bottom line. The more effectively and efficiently they managed the company's assets, the more value they created for their customers and for themselves.

When the owners of Matt Black Systems first devolved assets and liabilities down to each individual's P&L account, they saw an almost immediate 50% reduction in machinery within the factory. The workers rapidly sold off assets that were overpriced, underutilized, or unnecessary. They also took over management of the company's liabilities, negotiating far better terms and prices than their former administrators. They began to diligently maintain their existing equipment and to "sweat" the assets well after they were paid off and theoretically depreciated and used up. In short, they did more with less—and took pride in what they were able to accomplish.

Lastly, the large increase in productivity can be attributed to the equally large increase in authority the workers experienced under the new model. The powers of autonomy from the last chapter, coupled with managerial and administrative devolution, unleashed a powerful sense of agency that proved to be a productivity booster.

The owners of Matt Black Systems have developed a metaphor for the increase in authority and agency seen in the fractal model as compared to traditional command-and-control models. They liken it to the difference between stoplights and roundabouts.[8] Workers in a command-and-control hierarchy, they contend, are not unlike drivers subjected to stoplights. The lights tell drivers when to stop and when to go instead of leaving it up to the judgement of individual drivers.

Roundabouts, on the other hand, are like the fractal organizational model. They devolve the management of traffic down to the drivers themselves. Drivers in a roundabout are, in this sense, "self-leading." They dynamically collaborate with the other drivers in the roundabout to collectively manage the flow of traffic. The difference in efficacy between these two systems is stark. Roundabouts reduce fatal crashes by 90%, CO_2 emissions by 46%, and queue times by 65%.[9]

This is not unlike the difference Matt Black Systems has seen between their fractal model and the traditional command-and-control model. At Matt Black Systems, they've seen a 500% increase in productivity, as we've already seen, and they have enjoyed a 99% increase in quality (as measured by a drop in customer returns), a 98% increase in on-time deliveries, and a 97% increase in statutory and regulatory compliance.[10]

By turning every employee into a virtual company of one and devolving authority and responsibility to them, they have created a "self-leading" organization—where colleagues collectively navigate challenges and opportunities in real time.

Like Matt Black Systems, many of the pioneers in this book have devolved managerial authorities and responsibilities throughout their organizations. Although they have not gone so far as to give each individual their own personal profit-and-loss account, they have still dramatically increased the sense of ownership, stewardship, and authority among individuals within the organization.

Leadership Teams

Nearsoft is a truly radical organization that has developed a rich set of radically collaborative practices that we will encounter throughout this book, including the practice of *leadership teams*. To better understand how leadership teams work at Nearsoft, let's take a step back and learn a little bit about how this organization came to be. To do that, we have to understand why one of their founders, Matt Perez, decided to leave his successful corporate career track for a risky venture far from the beaten path.

By the late 1990s, Matt Perez was at a crossroads. On paper, he had a good career. He had worked at a variety of successful hardware and software startups. He'd enjoyed fancy titles, big salaries, and plenty of stock. Among his more impressive feats, he had run the Solaris Operating System division of Sun Microsystems during its heyday, when Solaris was the premier Unix operating system for enterprises around the world.

Despite all of this apparent success, something was wrong. The higher he climbed, the worse he felt. As he puts it, "I became worse as a boss and as a person. I was no longer the protector of people and had become the defender of my domain instead. I spent more time and effort looking out for number one and ended up not liking myself very much."[11]

By the time the dot-com bubble burst in the early 2000s, he had had enough. He could have continued leveraging his experiences and connections to climb the corporate ladder, but instead he vowed to get out of the hierarchy game altogether. And he saw just the business opportunity to make his exit with outsourcing.

By the early 2000s, outsourcing was all the rage in corporate America. After successfully outsourcing the Y2K bug fix to India, American executives thought, "If it works for a bug, it can work for any sort of software project." Of course, building a new software product or evolving an existing product is nothing like fixing a bug. Putting developers on the opposite side of the world from the business was a recipe for disaster.

As Perez notes, "Not being available to speak directly with each other was a killer. You couldn't resolve even simple questions in real time. Instead, a string of emails would fly back and forth, each one getting longer than the previous. Frustration would build up at both ends and what started as a small, simple question would become a major, complicated problem."[12]

Whatever money was saved in labor costs was lost in communication overhead and long cycle times—leading some businesses to abandon the idea of outsourcing altogether. Perez, however, reasoned that the problem wasn't outsourcing per se but *offshoring*. Instead of working with developers on the opposite end of the world, Perez thought, "Why not work with developers in Mexico?"

Unknown to most American executives, by the early 2000s Mexico had developed a budding software development industry eager to work with American companies. The time zones aligned so that Mexican software developers could work as full-fledged, dynamic participants on the team. Most Mexican developers were fluent in English and as a Cuban immigrant, Perez's first language was Spanish.

However, despite sharing a language, Perez admits, "I knew very little about Mexico, and what little I 'knew' was wrong."[13] His idea might never have gotten off the ground had he not met Roberto Martinez. At the time, Martinez ran a small bilingual software consultancy in Mexico, had experience with US clients, and, most importantly, shared Perez's desire to get out of the dominator hierarchy game. After a trial run of working together, they decided to go all in as cofounders.

When Perez and Martinez sat down to imagine their new US-to-Mexico outsourcing company, they drew up a list of "no" rules:

No bosses: They wanted a workplace where everyone "treated each other as adults" instead of a workplace where everyone had to "'pretty please' the boss for everything."[14] So they eliminated bosses—along with all of the associated euphemisms, like manager, leader, director, etc.

No employees: By eliminating bosses, they also eliminated something else they didn't want their new company to have: employees. That's because an employee is defined as a "person working for another person for pay"—which, as Doug Kirkpatrick, author of *The No-Limits Enterprise*, notes, is a concept that "is extraordinarily outdated . . . . Certainly, no millennial will tell you her life's goal is to labor for someone else when what she seeks is purpose and meaning to her work."[15] Instead of employees, Perez and Martinez created an organization of colleagues, whose relationships would be based on peer-to-peer equality instead of domination and coercion.

No titles: Next up on the chopping block: titles. As Perez writes, "A FIAT managed business is organized as a FIAT hierarchy where everybody is assigned a title by FIAT."[16] (*Fiat*, meaning "the power to give arbitrary orders," is Perez's unique way of describing a business organized as a static dominator hierarchy). Titles, they reasoned, are too intertwined with hierarchy, prestige, and power to be worth the trouble. If people wanted to give themselves a title, fine, but no one would have the power to bestow titles on others. Chop!

No secrets: In a hierarchical organization, a manager's power is, to a large degree, enabled by secrecy. Their ability to make decisions rests on information. If that information is widely known, then their decisions could be questioned and their decision-making power threatened. So Perez and Martinez decided that in their new company there would be no secrets. As Perez writes, "It is impossible to decentralize decision-making without the necessary information [being] transparent. And transparency without decentralization is simply frustrating, like seeing the candy behind that glass that you cannot reach."[17]

Now that they knew what they didn't want, all they had to figure out was what they *did* want. That, as it turned out, was easy. They wanted to build a company "in which everyone enjoyed their work and shared in the wealth."[18] So Nearsoft was born.

Aside from the above "no" rules, Nearsoft employees have been free to collectively work out the company's culture. To do that, they've developed a simple yet powerful practice for decentralized organizational governance known as leadership teams. To see now how leadership teams first developed and proved their mettle, we'll look at the thorniest of subjects: profit sharing.

In Nearsoft's early days, Martinez developed a formula for fairly distributing the company's dividends among all of its colleagues. It attempted to take into account things like tenure and an employee's relative contributions over the previous financial period. When Nearsoft was small, the formula was simple enough and satisfied most. However, as Nearsoft grew, the formula grew as well. Over the years, it became more and more complicated until eventually colleagues lost all faith in it.

In a typical organization, this wouldn't really matter. Employees would either have no insight into how profit distribution worked (if it even happened at all—a big "if") or they would have no ability to influence it. But as we've already seen, Nearsoft is far from typical.

A group of Nearsoft colleagues fed up with the formula decided to do something about it. They announced that they were creating a short-lived leadership team to come up with an alternative. They invited anyone interested in the topic to join. You read that correctly. Nearsoft's colleagues took ownership over a profit distribution policy previously owned by the CEO by simply saying that they were doing so.

Over the course of several weeks, this ad hoc team explored, discussed, and debated a number of different approaches. They consulted people inside and outside the organization. According to Perez, they treated it as a "below-the-waterline" decision[19]—the same metaphor that we have already seen at work at W. L. Gore. The decision, afterall, would affect everyone in the organization, and getting it wrong could be disastrous. In the end, they decided that the simplest approach was the best: divide the dividend equally among every single Nearsoft colleague.

This leadership team set a precedent. When someone wants to change something at Nearsoft, they simply announce that they want to do so and invite anyone else interested in the problem or in the solution to join them in an ad hoc leadership team. The teams themselves have no explicit rules for how to operate, other than they must abide by the relevant "no" rules of the company: in this case, the "no secrets" rule. So long as they are open to anyone and so long as they are transparent about what they discuss, what they decide, and why they decide it, they are free to change anything they see fit.

Leadership teams are an example of a devolutionary decision-making practice that enhances the spirit of collaboration while avoiding the grid-lock of consensus. Case in point: when the profit-sharing leadership team announced their decision to split the dividend equally, not everyone in the organization was happy with it. Some believed that their contribution should count more than others. But the decision proceeded despite the lack of unanimous support.

Rather than let the perfect be the enemy of the good, they moved forward with the new plan, knowing that if it didn't work out, a new leadership team could come together to try again. Furthermore, as one of their colleagues explained at the time, "We did as well as we did because of everybody. Trying to split hairs about specific contributions would be counterproductive. And who would be the judge of that?"[20]

Although it wasn't necessary to convince naysayers, this logic was in fact hard to argue with. Nearsoft is a consulting organization. The size and degree of everyone's contribution waxes and wanes, often for factors outside of anyone's individual control. It was their collective efforts that counted, leading to the company's overall success or failure. So long as everyone believed that everyone else was doing their level best, then an even distribution made sense.

The Devolution of Hiring (and Firing)

Who is best suited to determine whether or not someone should be hired or fired from an organization? Dominator hierarchies give these decisions to managers, directors, or even vice presidents. Radically collaborative organizations tend to have a different answer: the power to hire and fire should live with the makers themselves. That's because a radically collaborative organization believes that those who do the work are best able to determine if someone is capable of working with them.

At Haufe-umantis, for example, when a development team needs to grow, HR can source candidates for them but the team itself is left to look through the resumes and decide who to interview. It's also up to the team to run the interview, from culture fit to technical assessment, and to make a decision. While the team has the final say on whether or not to make an offer, if they reject someone, other teams are free to interview the candidate for themselves.

As Sergi Rodriguez, a Haufe developer, explained to me, "I have seen a team reject someone who was quite good technically but just didn't click personally. And then that same person was actually hired by another team. I like that, as a team, we have the last word on who joins us. If we don't click with a candidate, it's better to let another team try them out than to try to force something."

Devolving hiring power down to teams is a way to ensure that new hires actually fit in. And just because someone doesn't fit on one team doesn't mean they wouldn't fit in on another. Giving teams the power to interview candidates that other teams reject can mitigate the possibility that someone would be unduly turned down for a job.

One telling side effect of decentralizing hiring power to the teams is that referrals increase dramatically. Mark Stoffel, the former CEO of Haufe-umantis, explains the impact that they experienced when they devolved hiring power to the teams: "In the previous situation, only 5% of the new hires were recruited through referrals, despite having a very generous referring policy. Now, in the new situation, 60% of new hires are recruited through referrals!"[21]

As makers begin to take more ownership over the hiring process, they begin to source candidates themselves. I've seen this process play out first-hand. Although Pivotal Labs, the agile consulting company, became an increasingly hierarchical organization during my eight-year tenure there, the frontline employees retained a good deal of control over the hiring process. When I became Head of Engineering, I began to meet with our internal recruiting teams who shared stats with me on referrals. They were astonishing.

In several of our offices around the world, pivots (as Pivotal employees were known) referred candidates at rates an order of magnitude above the industry average. And it wasn't hard to see why. Despite the rapidly growing dominator hierarchy, of which I was a part, pivots still radically collaborated as much as they could. Their ways of working were structured and regimented through Extreme Programming practices like pair programming and test-driven development, yet those practices were collaborative and intimate in nature and based on a paradigm of partnership and equality. So when teams and offices needed to grow, the consultants themselves naturally began to refer people that they would enjoy radically collaborating with, like former coworkers, friends, and even family. They loved what they did, and they wanted others who they cared about to experience it too.

Of course, no hiring process is perfect, and sometimes people who join an organization simply don't work out. Sometimes it's just a case of being in the wrong role. In this situation, practices like autonomy of role can help solve the problem. Or sometimes they're dealing with personal issues outside of work that are affecting their performance inside of work. Deficiency-gratifying workplaces, as we'll see in Chapter 5, tend to be capable of rectifying this situation too.

But sometimes, despite everyone's best efforts, someone doesn't work out and no change of role or personal situation will change that fact. They simply need to be fired. But who is capable of making that call? Nearsoft has a simple answer: teams.

Teams at Nearsoft have the power to fire one of their team members if they believe that team member is irreparably underperforming or unforgivably misbehaving. After exhausting every other approach they deem possible, team members can band together and decide to remove someone from the organization entirely. When this happens, Nearsoft has developed a specific culture for what to do in the aftermath of a firing.

The team, after firing one of their colleagues, announces it to the entire company and invites anyone interested to a Q&A about the situation. As one colleague there, Nyx Zamora, explained to me,

> The team has to stand in front of their colleagues and explain their decision and what they did to try to avoid firing them. The questions

can be really intense. But this is the fairest process I've seen. It's not a single individual or manager making the decision. It's your colleagues, and there's a process, there's communication, and there's accountability.

According to Perez, this has only happened three times in all of Nearsoft's existence—a testament to Nearsoft's hiring processes and to its caring and collaborative culture.

From Workplace Democracy to Self-Management

AT A GLANCE

Haufe-umantis: Collaboration and talent management software company. Employs two hundred people. Founded in 2002. Based in Switzerland. Notable for transitioning from dominator hierarchy to workplace democracy to self-management/radical collaboration.

If you could change the software that companies use to recruit and manage employees, could you change the way business works? That was the bet that Hermann Arnold made back in 2001 when he founded the software company umantis. He was on a mission to "fix the traditional way of working,"[22] and he began with talent management software.

Initially, Arnold's bet seemed to pay off. Within a short amount of time, a growing number of businesses began to use the umantis talent management system. Revenue quickly grew—and so did the umantis workforce. But that growth led to communication and coordination complexity. So, umantis did what any other company did in their situation: they hired managers. And when that didn't work, they did what any other company did next: they hired senior managers. But, of course, that didn't really work either. Communication and coordination challenges remained, while innovation and entrepreneurship plummeted.[23]

Despite their ideals, umantis seemed in danger of becoming that which they had set out to change: a traditional company. So they did something unexpected. They voted.

The vote came about during a crisis. In 2008, the US economy faltered, triggering a global recession. Companies around the world stopped hiring. Unsurprisingly, umantis's business plummeted. Arnold and the management team considered doing what other bureaucratic management teams around the world were already doing: mass layoffs. But to Arnold, this would have been the final nail in his idealistic coffin.

Instead, he assembled the entire company together, explained the direness of the situation, and asked everyone to vote. Either they lay off a significant number of the workforce or they all take significant pay cuts until the economy bounced back. The employees overwhelmingly chose the latter and the company survived the recession with jobs intact.[24]

This single vote began a years-long transformation process that continues to this day. The first stage of their transformation was democratization. Significant decisions within the company were no longer decided by managers alone—instead, they were put to a vote.

For example, the umantis workforce voted against merging with a large competitor whose culture was the antithesis of theirs. But they voted for merging with a somewhat smaller competitor whose mission and culture did reflect their own, leading to the company's current name: Haufe-umantis.[25]

They also began to elect their leaders, starting with the CEO and eventually expanding to all of their leadership positions, on a yearly basis. Leaders would put together campaign platforms with new visions for how the company could work. Employees then selected leaders based on the strength of their visions and plans.

Democracy worked for this stage of growth. As their former CEO Mark Stoffel explained, democratic decision-making brought a much-needed clarity to the workforce: "Employees study the situation and pose queries before they make judgement calls."[26]

Instead of managers making decisions behind closed doors, the company as a whole was able to explore, debate, and decide on the important issues of the day. Stoffel also described a new sense of motivation created by elections: "Because [employees] are actively involved, they are usually able to accept any outcome. We vote to follow a certain direction and are naturally motivated to ensure that it works."[27] When employees elect a leader based on the strength of that leader's vision, they have a vested interest in seeing that vision come to fruition. In this way, elections became a motivational force within the company.

But nothing lasts forever. Although workplace democracy worked for a while, it eventually failed to scale with the company. For starters, it failed logistically. Elections require communication, planning, and coordination. When Haufe-umantis was in a single office with a single colocated workforce, those logistics were manageable. But as they began to open multiple offices throughout Europe, the election process grew unwieldy. Employees in one location struggled to understand candidates from another location, since they had little to no face-to-face interaction with them.

Furthermore, over the years elections led to unintended side effects. Employees, for instance, began to avoid dealing with leadership problems as they occurred, instead hoping that the next election would fix it. As Arnold points out, this unintended consequence "reversed an important advantage of the elections, namely the increase in leadership quality."[28]

Finally, workplace democracy isn't as radical as it sounds. At the end of the day, when the ballots are tallied and the new leaders made official, the result is still a dominator hierarchy. As Arnold lamented, "Elected superiors are part of a particularly prominent hierarchy, which increasingly contradicts today's demands on agile companies."[29]

And as Axel Singler, a long-time Haufe-umantis employee, told me in an interview, "Elections are about fighting for power—not with weapons but with words and regulations. But a company should not fight for power. A company has a clear stakeholder, owner, and purpose, and all the people should be aligned on that."

Democracy seemed to have run its course at Haufe-umantis. So what did they do? They did what any democratic workplace would do: they democratically elected a nine-person employee council to democratically determine an alternative to democracy.

Over the course of six months, that council explored alternative organizational models. With the help of four external consultants, they looked at the ways other radical organizations worked and what kind of practices they used for making decisions. One of those consultants was Frederic Laloux, who in 2014 published *Reinventing Organizations*.

As part of his research for that book, Laloux discovered a number of non-hierarchical organizations that used something known as the *advice process*. The advice process effectively empowers everyone in the organization to make any decision provided they first ask the advice of those who could be affected by the decision. Among all of the alternatives that the council considered, this one rose above the rest.

As Arnold explains, "What we particularly liked about this method is that the quality of decisions can be significantly improved in this way and that employees are even more involved."[30]

So in June of 2019, the company adopted the advice process and began the next stage of their evolution—from democracy to self-management; from employees as "voters" to employees as "decision makers."

Today, Haufe-umantis is a company in transition. As Singler explained to me, they are inspired by the idea that "although AI may soon be better than humans at many things, collaboration is a uniquely human ability." They're on a mission to help people and teams improve the quality and impact of their collaborations. To that end, they're creating—and dogfooding—collaboration software. Their newfound purpose, coupled with their transformation toward autonomy and self-management, has converged into a promising future for Haufe-umantis that we explore throughout this book.

The Advice Process

When Haufe-umantis decided workplace democracy had run its course at their organization, they replaced it with a self-managing organizational practice known as the *advice process*. This process is both radical and radically simple: allow anyone in the organization to make any decision so long as they seek the advice of those affected. The more people affected, the more advice they must seek—and yet they are under no obligation to *take* anyone's advice.

There are no specific rules for how advice must be solicited; it could be as informal as off-the-cuff, one-on one conversations or as deliberate as a well-researched presentation to a large audience with surveys for feedback. In several of the organizations featured within this book, this process is open to everyone within the organization for a wide array of decisions, from simple changes in team practices to complex multimillion-dollar investments. Let's look at where this practice first originated before seeing how it operates at scale.

The advice process can be traced back to Applied Energy Services, Inc. (now known as AES Corporation), a global energy company that garnered intense interest in the 1990s for its radical workplace culture. The founders, Dennis Bakke and Roger Sant, created the company with an atypical goal in mind. They weren't set on riches or competitive domination. Instead, they wanted to create a workplace that let everyone experience joy in their daily lives. Bakke and Sant were fed up with uninspiring and demoralizing workplaces, and they were convinced that it was not only possible but vital for businesses to find ways of working that enriched human experience. There was just one problem: they didn't know how to do that.

During a recent interview with Modern Servant Leader, Bakke recounted a pivotal moment early on in the AES story.[31] Although he and his power plant were in the United States, his board was based in Geneva, Switzerland. He found himself going into the plant in the middle of the night to have phone calls with the board. On one of these late-night jaunts, he wandered around chatting with the skeleton crew that manned the power plant during the wee hours. With so few people, the atmosphere was relaxed and intimate.

One of the employees showed a calendar to Bakke hung up on the wall. It was an unusual calendar, for each page of the calendar was an entire year. And when the employee flipped the calendar thirty years into the future, Blake saw little red circles sprinkled about the pages.

"What are those?" asked Bakke.

The employee told him that the conditions at the plant were so demoralizing that after a few months of working here new employees would circle a date thirty years into the future representing the date that they could finally retire with a pension.

Bakke was horrified. He and Sant had tried to create the conditions for joy in their fledgling power plant enterprise, but instead of joy, the workplace was one of dread, and the dreams of the workforce were dreams of escape. He resolved then and there to discover and root out the underlying disease that afflicted their workplace. He eventually found the root cause: the traditional command-and-control organizational structure and what we now know as a dominator hierarchy.

Bakke decided that command-and-control organizations inhibit joy at work because they withhold decision-making power. As he explained, "the main thing that distinguishes us from animals is our ability to think, reason, make decisions, and hold ourselves responsible."[32] How could people experience joy in their lives if their environment robbed them of their most human abilities?

He decided that his job as CEO was "to maximize the number of chances for people in the workplace to make decisions and hold themselves responsible—because that's what will lead to joy at work."[33] Over the years, Bakke, Sant, and the rest of the workforce experimented with different forms of decentralized decision-making until they eventually arrived at the advice process as described above. Frontline power plant employees throughout the company began to take control of their work and workplaces and to involve themselves in cross-functional aspects of the business, like finance. And academic institutions and newspaper organizations at the time began to take notice.

Frederic Laloux dug up an article in the *Wall Street Journal* from that era that begins with this eyebrow-raising image of managerial devolution at AES: "His hands still blackened from coal he has just unloaded from a barge, Jeff Hatch picks up the phone and calls his favorite broker. 'What kind of rate can you give me for $10 million at 30 days?' he asks the agent, who handles treasury bills. 'Only 6.09? But I just got a 6.13 quote from Chase.'"[34]

That's right—the same laborer who slung coal was also managing multi-million-dollar investments. That's because by utilizing the advice process, AES had slowly and methodically devolved managerial and administrative responsibilities throughout the organization. They found that employees who other companies had simply written off as "unskilled" labor actually relished the opportunity to manage assets and make big decisions. And they were surprisingly effective at it. They didn't shy away from leveling up their financial acumen. And what's more, the added responsibilities gave them a sense of ownership over the organization that created the authentic conditions for joy at work—the initial goal that Bakke and Sant had set out to achieve.

Since being introduced at AES, a number of organizations around the world have begun to practice the advice process, including radically collaborative pioneers Buurtzorg, Johnsonville Sausage, and W. L. Gore, as well as other organizations, like FAVI, the prestigious French automotive parts manufacturer, and Sun Hydraulics, the leading designer and manufacturer of high-performance fluid power systems.

Other organizations, while not adopting it wholesale, have still adapted it to their circumstances. For example, Nearsoft's leadership teams are, in practice, a type of modified advice process. By announcing a problem to solve and inviting anyone interested to be a part of the solution, advice becomes an opt-in affair.

As Haufe-umantis has begun to incorporate the advice process into their organization over the past couple of years, they have noticed the biggest change of behavior among leadership. As a reminder, leadership at Haufe-umantis used to be elected. And although the organization put most significant company decisions to a vote during their company's democratic phase, leaders there could still make somewhat smaller decisions by fiat.

The advice process, however, has led to a shift in mindset among Haufe-umantis leaders. As Axel Singler explained to me,

> With the advice process, every employee can, in principle, decide anything. They just have to make sure that they ask the affected people and the people who have the most knowledge in that area. In practice, 90% of the advice process is from leaders. It's been a process of strengthening our mindset that you should not decide out of your leadership role, you should decide based on asking those affected by your decision, and by asking experts.

If Singler could change anything about the implementation of the advice process at Haufe-umantis so far, he said he would change the name, because the word "process" has been sullied by laborious bureaucracies. He continued,

> When some employees hear "advice process," all they actually hear is "process." If I could turn back the clock, I would call it the advice *mindset*, because at its core, the advice process is a mindset deeply aligned with our own organizational purpose. It fosters collaboration and communication so that we can all come to better decisions. This is the core of its value.

Holacracy-Powered Devolution

In order to devolve managerial power and authority throughout their organization, cLabs chose to implement Holacracy. That's because, at heart, Holacracy is a framework for radically collaborative organizational governance.

In Holacracy, there are no managers who sit on high, commanding subordinates, controlling salaries, conducting performance reviews, or designing organizational structures. Instead, managers are replaced with a rules-based system for collectively defining and iterating on roles, for investing those roles with autonomy and self-management, and for giving everyone in the organization the power to alter, adapt, and innovate on the organization's structure. Whether it's someone filling out a janitorial role and sensing a conflict between that role and the role that procures cleaning supplies, or someone filling out the product manager role sensing a misalignment between sales and R&D, Holacracy gives everyone the power to elevate organizational tensions and to rapidly resolve them without resorting to consensus.

Before we look at how this process works, it's important to understand this focus on decentralized resolution of organizational tensions (i.e., conflicts originating in misalignments between roles and departments) stems directly from the frustration that Holacracy's founder, Brian J. Robertson, experienced while working in traditional organizational hierarchies. As he wrote in his book, *Holacracy*, within hierarchical organizations,

> Most [organizational] tensions sensed by individuals . . . simply have nowhere to go. Tensions are just not recognized as among the organization's greatest resources. When I realized that my boss wasn't able to make use of my human capacity to sense and respond, I did the only logical thing: I became a boss myself. Now I could really process whatever it was I sensed, right? Well, there was still a higher boss to act as a bottleneck, and another, and another.[35]

No matter how high Robertson climbed, the problem remained—even when he left those organizations to found his own company. As he lamented,

> The sheer lack of hours in a day became a limiting factor: there was far too much complexity landing on my desk for the organization to fully harness even my own consciousness as its CEO. And that wasn't the worst of it. The more painful realization was that I had built just the kind of system I had worked for so long to get out of. Everyone who worked for me was in the same position I had been in.[36]

At this point, he knew that it was time to get out of the hierarchy game altogether. After many years of experimentation with a group of fellow pioneers, he crystallized a radically collaborative organizational framework and christened it *Holacracy*.

The term is based on the root word "holon," meaning "a whole within a larger whole." As Robertson notes, "Each cell in your body is a holon—both a self-contained, whole entity and a part of a larger whole, an organ. In the same way, each organ is itself a self-contained whole yet also a part of a larger whole."[37] In other words, your body is a sort of Holacracy—a nested set of self-organizing, autonomous systems that nonetheless work together to compose your physical being. And your organization can function on just the same organizing principle.

Holacracy-powered organizations are structured as nested sets of circles—with each circle consisting of roles, supercircles, and subcircles. For example, a small software-as-a-service company might consist of circles like development and marketing, with roles like software developer and social media promoter, respectively. Each role, in turn, consists of high-level goals. A social media promoter might have the goal: "create and maintain a highly engaged social media community."

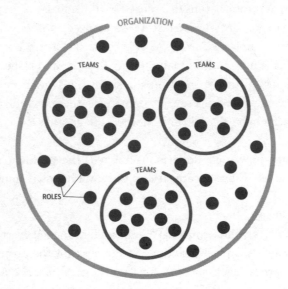

Figure 3: Holacracy-Powered Organizational Structure

So far, this may not sound all that different from any other organizational structure—until you consider the fact that roles in Holacracy are *self-managing* and circles are *self-organizing*. Let's look at these facets in turn.

As we saw in the last chapter, roles within Holacracy are, by definition, *self-managing*. When someone accepts a role within a Holacracy-powered organization, they commit to fulfill that role's high-level goals, but the choice of *how* to achieve those goals lies entirely with them. There's no manager or boss who can tell someone how to achieve a role's goals or when to achieve them by.

Instead, each individual role filler is given the autonomy to choose what they do, how they do it, and when they do it on any given day. When you accept a role within a Holacracy-powered organization, you make a commitment to everyone within the organization to do your utmost to achieve the goals associated with the role. This commitment creates a sense of peer-to-peer accountability, similar to the commitments and accountabilities we experience in everyday life.

Think about it like this: outside of work, you freely make commitments to others—like your families, your neighbors, and your friends—and you are naturally accountable for those commitments because failing to honor your commitments has tangible consequences on both you and on those who depend on you. The real difference between accountability in a Holacracy-powered organization versus accountability in daily life is this: in daily, social life it is hard to change a structural impediment that impacts your ability to honor your commitments.

If you are, for instance, committed to providing for your family but are turned down for roles because of systemic discrimination, you will likely have to struggle long and hard to rectify this situation. But in a Holacracy-powered organization, it is *easy* to address a structural impediment that limits your ability to honor the commitments you make within the organization. That's because you, along with every other member of the organization, have a built-in framework for rapidly adapting, altering, and evolving the organization's structure in order to better achieve outcomes. This is the *self-organizing* nature of Holacracy, and the specific Holacracy-powered process that enables it is called governance.

Governance meetings are the nonhierarchical building block of a Holacracy-powered organization. They take place within any and every circle in the organization, and they provide a space for anyone within a circle to raise up a tension and have it quickly processed. Processing a tension could result in new or redistributed role accountabilities, new policies, new roles, even new circles altogether. Processing a tension can also dissolve goals, roles, policies, and circles entirely.

The rules for conducting governance meetings are rigorous and won't be learned overnight. But for anyone who has struggled long and hard to effect even the smallest change within a hierarchical organization, a Holacracy-powered governance meeting can seem like magic.

As Robertson writes,

> Back in the days with my software company, I remember a governance meeting of our General Company circle that had been scheduled for a two-hour slot. In this meeting, we changed our

salary system quite dramatically, restructured part of the organization in a major way, and adopted a few new policies that affected the whole organization. None of these topics were discussed or "socialized" before the meeting. We finished half an hour early, and everybody involved had fully bought into the path forward. . . .

As the meeting was closing, the facilitator offered an apology for being a little off his game: he felt that the meeting had taken longer than necessary. Others agreed. It wasn't until we were leaving the room that it occurred to me how unusual this was compared to most organizations—look what we had accomplished in ninety minutes. But in an organization that has mastered Holacracy, this rapid restructuring and integration is the norm.[38]

This is the self-organizing promise of Holacracy—an organization that collectively senses and responds to organizational tensions and that rapidly harnesses the energy within those tensions to propel the organization forward.

Even with the power to collectively and continuously devolve authority throughout an organization—either through simple practices like the advice process or through rules-based procedures like the Holacracy-powered governance process—there's still the overarching problem of cultivating a self-management mindset.

Radically Collaborative Onboarding

Baggage. That's what most of us would bring with us if we were lucky enough to join a radically collaborative organization. Our past experiences in dominator hierarchies weigh us down, color our interactions, and limit our perception of what's possible. In fact, many of us have been downright traumatized—emotionally and psychologically—by these past experiences, creating a significant challenge for our integration into a radically collaborative organization. Thankfully, several of the radically collaborative pioneers featured within this book have recognized this challenge and can offer patterns for acclimating new people.

New employees at Nearsoft, for example, begin their journey to self-management and radical collaboration by exploring what "freedom" means during their initial onboarding. As a reminder, Nearsoft's motto is "freedom in the workplace," and their experiences have more than lived up to the radical implications that that motto signifies. But few new hires at Nearsoft have any real experience with a freedom-based workplace, so they need help internalizing it.

As Iris Hernandez, a Nearsoft colleague who has spearheaded support programs for employees for the last five years, told me, "We have several trainings to help colleagues understand what a freedom-based culture is, how it works, and what you need to identify in yourself to thrive within it. It begins with the word *freedom* itself—which we take to mean the freedom to make decisions and to be responsible and accountable for the decisions you make."

In other words, Nearsoft doesn't start with behaviors or practices—they begin with individual mindset.

Nearsoft's definition of freedom, although intended to be empowering to new hires, can also be scary. There's a certain comfort in taking orders and abdicating responsibility like most people do within dominator hierarchies—albeit a comfort that Nearsoft sees no value in. When I asked Hernandez how she helps people get over their fears, her answer was surprising: "We don't. Freedom is not working without fear. It's working in spite of fear. And for that, people need to understand themselves."

That's why part of Nearsoft's support programs focus on helping people reflect on the source of their fears, since, as Hernandez puts it, that source is what "holds them back from being responsible and making a decision." Freedom in the workplace, as it turns out, is as much about the individual as it is about the organization. For an individual to practice freedom in the workplace, they must first set themselves free.

At a lot of corporations, onboarding programs tend to be run by HR departments divorced from the actual work of the company, and they are quickly forgotten about, since they have little bearing on the day-to-day work of the employee. But at Nearsoft, the people programs that begin during onboarding do not end until a colleague leaves the organization entirely. "We're with you from your first day to your last," Hernandez says.

In addition to trainings that help people cultivate a freedom-based mindset, Hernandez's team has also codesigned trainings to help people learn how to self-solicit the perspectives of their peers, how to chart a personal growth path, even how to craft role change and career change plans. Nearsoft's approach to support is holistic and inseparable from the rest of the Nearsoft culture.

Nearsoft isn't the only pioneer to recognize the need to quickly orient newcomers into their radically decentralized culture. When TIM Group transitioned from hierarchy to heterarchy, they too recognized this need.

To that end, they borrowed a practice from one of their self-managing archetypes, W. L. Gore.

New hires at W. L. Gore initially struggled to find their way within the self-organizing innovation organization. As one new hire put it, "I didn't know who did what. I wondered how anything got done here. It was driving me crazy."[39]

So colleagues at Gore began volunteering to "sponsor" new hires. These sponsors would show new hires around the organization, help them get to know individuals, teams, and practices, and answer their questions. They would also correct—repeatedly, if necessary—new hires who attempted to map their hierarchical experiences and expectations onto the organization. For example, when one new hire asked "Who's my boss?" their sponsor had to repeatedly tell them that they have no boss.

> *New hire:* "Secretly, there are bosses, right?"
> *Sponsor:* "Stop saying the B-word!"[40]

Old habits do indeed die hard.

New hires at TIM Group found themselves in a similar predicament as new hires at W. L. Gore, so the developers at TIM Group created a Gore-inspired practice called "onboarding buddies." An onboarding buddy would help new hires adjust to their newfound autonomies, like autonomy of allocation.

As Graham Allan, a former TIM Group developer, explained to me, "It was the onboarding buddy's job to introduce the new hire to everything, including deciding what team they wanted to join and what they wanted to work on."

How long that took varied. Andy Parker, a TIM Group developer, explained that some new hires would choose a team within hours, while others would spend days shopping around, so to speak: "New hires would pair-program with different teams to get a feel for the possibilities." At that point, the team would take over and help the new hire adjust to further dimensions of autonomy, like autonomy of practice.

The development arm of TIM Group found the onboarding buddy practice valuable, but they also found the process behind the practice just as valuable. Anyone within the organization could easily become an onboarding buddy because everyone who played the role also helped craft the documentation around the role. The documents became a source of both collective role design and collective wisdom.

As Jeffrey Fredrick explained, "Problems like onboarding are shared problems that we all have a joint interest in solving, so we should jointly design the solutions. That's the principle behind self-management." This idea of shared problems and shared solutions became a guiding light for devolving managerial responsibilities throughout their organization.

Conclusion

As our pioneers prove, there's no inherent reason that management has to be left to managers. Managerial powers and responsibilities can be devolved into the organization as a whole, without watering down that power and without succumbing to the pitfalls of consensus. Teams and individuals can effectively manage the organization themselves—and increase their sense of ownership, stewardship, and authority in the process.

As we have seen, this is a productivity booster. But it's also an evolutionary amplifier. Devolved organizations *evolve* faster than static dominator hierarchies. That's because they give everyone in the organization the ability to sense *and respond* to tensions within the organizational structure, thereby unleashing the evolutionary potential of the organization as a whole.

There's one form of managerial devolution that we have yet to consider—and it's a doozy. How do devolved organizations handle that most intimate of matters, an individual's salary? This is a complex problem with ramifications beyond the organization. In most Western cultures, an individual's social status is tightly bound to their individual net worth. Salary becomes a way to connect individuals and organizations into the larger dominator hierarchies within society at large. Detangling this connection is a must for radically collaborative organizations. So in the next chapter, we'll take an in-depth look at the flaws, bias, and coercion behind traditional salary methods. And we'll also look at the radically collaborative alternatives that are beginning to gain momentum in the world.

Questions for Reflection

» When TIM Group began to devolve management out of the hands of a dominator hierarchy and into the the hands of a self-managing heterarchy, they began by devolving their line manager role. If you were to begin a devolutionary process within your organization, where would you start?

» This chapter detailed a number of devolutionary management practices, like ad hoc leadership teams, the advice process, Holacracy-powered governance, and devolved hiring and firing. Which of these practices would be easiest to introduce into your organization? Which would be hardest? Why?

» TIM Group's transformation from hierarchy to heterarchy was precipitated by a reading group. Instead of an "enlightened" manager dictating a devolutionary transformation to everyone "for their own good," the developers at TIM Group came to devolution on their own terms and ran with the ideas behind it of their own volition. How could you bring about a radically collaborative devolution within your organization without forcing the idea on anyone else?

CHAPTER 4

IMPERATIVE #2 CONTINUED: THE DEVOLUTION OF COMPENSATION

In the last chapter, we looked at the devolution of management along a number of dimensions, including leadership, hiring, firing, and governance. But there's one dimension of managerial devolution that we have yet to cover: the devolution of compensation. How our compensation is determined—and who determines it—has a significant impact not only on organizational performance but also on individual well-being. No discussion of radically collaborative devolution would be complete without an examination of this topic—and the topic is extensive enough, and foundational enough, that I've devoted this entire chapter to it.

The predominant compensation method found in organizations today is the annual performance appraisal, in which managers evaluate and rank their employees and make compensation adjustments based on those rankings on a yearly basis. Among organizations structured as dominator hierarchies, this method is widely implemented and widely maligned.

For example, YouGov, a global market research and data analytics firm, recently found that only 26% of employees associate performance evaluations with the term "useful." The remaining 74% associate it with terms like "time-consuming," "pointless," and "stressful."[1]

Likewise, Gartner, the global research organization, found that a full 96% of managers are dissatisfied with the annual performance appraisal process.[2] Coupled with another finding that, on average, a full 60% of a manager's rating is attributable to the subjective beliefs and biases of the manager, as opposed to any objective assessment of the employee being rated,[3] it becomes hard to imagine a more problematic way to manage compensation.

Let's look at just a few real-life accounts of how arbitrary and painful this process can be for employees:

After six and a half years and five strong/positive performance reviews, my company made some changes and hired a new person as my manager, while my former manager had another role. After four months, my new manager gave me my review, which was not even close to my historical reviews. I asked if he had consulted my former manager and was told: "After a few months, I'm comfortable I know you well enough to not have to consult anyone."[4]

In one of the organizations that I worked in, we were asked to fill out pages of answers to open-ended subjective questions. We did. Only to find out later that our manager had already filled in his ratings before he left for a vacation a week before we started writing the reviews. Our painstakingly written responses had absolutely no purpose apart from making us feel like we were writing something up.[5]

I was told that no one could score over a 3 (out of 5) this year because we had too much change to cope with . . . I over exceeded all my targets and spent £40k less than the previous year to achieve this. I feel a bit like companies of a certain size use them [reviews] as a means of not giving people the pay raises they deserve. A previous example is being told that "We can't increase your salary this year as you only scored a 3 on your end of year."[6]

I was told that "someone" at "a meeting" "somewhere, sometime" didn't like my facial expressions, and that I needed to make sure my facial expressions were nicer. My manager could not define which meeting, who said it, where it was, or when.[7]

I was told I was "too direct" in my communications. To this day I still have no idea what that meant. When I asked for clarification as to what I was supposed to do differently in communicating with people—was I supposed to be more indirect?—they couldn't tell me specifics. I got the feeling [that] asking directly for clear, unambiguous feedback rubbed them the wrong way.[8]

I was told I was 'too polite' in my interactions with others. When I asked for an example of how I could improve, I was told to "say please and thank you less often." It was another long year before I could get out of there.[9]

This situation is a calamity for organizations. When managers mete out compensation adjustments based on their subjective judgements, biases, and beliefs, they diminish morale and productivity and breed resentment against bosses and competition among peers. Likewise, when managers dangle promotions, bonuses, and raises in front of us in exchange for our compliance with their demands, they distract us from the creativity, innovation, and entrepreneurship that we are otherwise capable of. Managerial control over compensation is one of the biggest barriers to radical collaboration within an organization—and so it is imperative that compensation be devolved out of the hands of a static dominator hierarchy and into the hands of a self-organizing, dynamic heterarchy.

Radically collaborative organizations around the world are already pioneering new, devolved compensation systems that we'll explore in this chapter. They're eliminating managerial control, coercion, and bias from the compensation process. And as we'll soon see, they're proving that not only can compensation be effectively handled without hierarchical control, but also that its devolution can have positive second-order effects on individual well-being and creative collaboration.

However, before we survey these devolved compensation practices, we'll first take a moment to debunk the two basic myths of managerial compensation control: the *myth of necessity* and the *myth of objectivity*. These myths are widespread among managers and employees alike, and belief in them is used to prop up and justify hierarchical control of compensation. In order to successfully move beyond coercive compensation systems, we have to lay bare the lies behind these myths. In doing so, we can better understand the real source of human motivation and the devolved compensation methods that follow from it.

Debunking the Myths of Managerial Compensation

People, primarily management, are quick to defend dominator hierarchies, and nowhere is this more evident than when discussing the managerial control of pay. People vehemently balk at the mere suggestion of devolving the control of salaries out of the hands of managers and into the workforce as a whole. The idea strikes them as preposterous, impossible—even utopian.

Historically, there has been a class-based assumption in our society that human beings are inherently lazy and unmotivated and will only perform well when coerced with carrots and sticks, rewards and punishments. This assumption was exposed in the 1950s by the MIT professor Douglas McGregor and later popularized in his landmark management book, *The Human Side of Enterprise*. In management theory, it is formally known as *Theory X*, where "X" represents a sort of pictorial mnemonic for a worker crossing their arms in an "X" shape, thus signaling a refusal to work.[10]

The belief behind Theory X is often tacit. People pick it up little by little from the offhand comments of family and friends, from the behaviors and attitudes of bosses and coworkers, and from the situations and plots of books and movies. Although most people will never consciously formulate the concept to themselves or put it into words, it will nonetheless color their beliefs, observations, and behaviors.

The Myth of Necessity

Theory X is the basis for the first myth of managerial compensation control: *the myth of necessity*. According to this myth, managers must control workers with rewards and punishments, like raises, bonuses, and performance evaluations. If human beings are inherently lazy and recalcitrant, as Theory X would have us believe—if they will cross their arms and refuse to work unless they are poked and prodded into action—then of course it is necessary for managers to control pay. If they didn't, nothing would ever get done. Without externally controlled incentives, workers would just sit back and draw a paycheck, never lifting so much as a finger to do any real work.

There's only one real problem with Theory X: it's false. Seventy-five years of research into human behavior has begun to reveal a very different picture of motivation. What scientists and researchers into the human condition have discovered is that human beings are naturally, intrinsically motivated—that left to their own devices they won't sit still like inert blobs as Theory X would have us believe. Instead, they'll pursue interests with passion and even dogged determination.

As Abraham Maslow, whose groundbreaking research into motivation in the mid-twentieth century changed the way we understand human behavior, proclaimed in the 1960s, "All the evidence that we have indicates that in practically every human being, and certainly in almost every newborn baby, there is an active will toward the actualization of human potentialities."[11]

And as Edward Deci, one of the most influential motivational research-ers of the twentieth century succinctly summarized in 1999 after an intense meta-analysis of over fifty years of research, "Intrinsic motiva-tion is an inherent motivational tendency."[12] Unfortunately, although it is inborn and instinctoid, our "active will" toward mastery and the realization of our "human potentialities" is "weak and delicate and subtle and easily overcome."[13] It can be attenuated, even destroyed, by carrots and sticks, domination and coercion.

As Deci explains,

> The evidence indicates clearly that strategies that focus primarily on the use of extrinsic rewards do, indeed, run a serious risk of diminishing rather than promoting intrinsic motivation . . . . When institutions—families, schools, businesses, and athletic teams, for example—focus on the short term and opt for controlling people's behavior, they may be having a substantially negative long-term effect.[14]

And as Daniel Pink brutally summarizes in his 2009 bestseller, *Drive: The Surprising Truth About What Motivates Us*, "carrots and sticks extin-guish intrinsic motivation; diminish performance; crush creativity; crowd out good behavior; encourage cheating, shortcuts, and unethical behavior; become addictive; and foster short-term thinking."[15]

In other words, Theory X is a self-fulfilling prophecy. If you manage people according to the belief that they are inherently lazy and will only perform well when extrinsically motivated, you will eventually create a workforce that conforms to that very belief because you will diminish and eventually destroy any intrinsic motivation people had for their work.

Although I will illustrate a few basic results from the field of motiva-tion theory below, I want to make it clear that it is not the purpose of this book to give you a comprehensive survey of this fascinating field that is psychological research. Nonetheless, I do want to give you a small window into this world now so that you may begin to understand the underlying psychology that helps explain the destructive effects of managerial com-pensation control.

The first bit of research involves the counterintuitive effects that rewards and punishments have on performance. Theory X would have us believe that incentives and disincentives are necessary to increase per-formance. That students must be rewarded with good grades and special privileges in order to motivate them to learn or that workers must be given performance evaluations with compensation strings attached in order to motivate and ensure performance improvements. Yet researchers have found, across a wide range of contexts, age ranges, cultures, and eras, that incentives like these *reduce* performance levels in their potential recipients. Here's a few of the more memorable studies that can begin to make sense of this counterintuitive effect.

In an early study of the effects of incentives on creativity and performance, 128 adults were individually presented with a box of matches, a box of thumbtacks, and a small candle, and told to mount the candle to the wall using only these materials. The solution, which required a little "outside of the box" creativity, was to empty the boxes and then use the thumbtacks to mount one of the boxes to the wall so that the candle could be placed on top of it. Half of the study participants were offered money in exchange for a correct solution, while the other half were promised nothing. According to Theory X, the half offered money should have performed better. Instead, they took 50% *longer* to solve the problem.[16]

In a similar study, a group of adults were asked to "select the pattern on each page that was least like the other two patterns on that page."[17] Again, half the participants were offered monetary incentives for correct answers while the other half were offered nothing. And again, the group offered nothing performed better—even when the monetary rewards were doubled for the other group.[18]

A group of fledgling journalists were observed while learning how to craft headlines according to their newspaper's specific rules. Some of these journalists were offered monetary incentives for each headline they produced while others were not incentivized. The quality of headlines among those rewarded plateaued, while the quality of those not rewarded continued to improve. Once again, rewards *reduced* performance.[19]

A group of artists were judged on the quality of their work. Each artist offered both commissioned and non-commissioned pieces for judgement, which were then reviewed by an independent panel of professional artists who neither knew whose pieces they were evaluating nor whether the pieces were commissioned or noncommissioned. The commissioned pieces—those produced for a monetary reward negotiated in advance— were deemed to be of lower quality.[20]

Although I've only teased a handful of studies here, know that they aren't outliers. There are dozens and dozens of studies from the field of experimental psychology like these, conducted all over the world over the course of decades. They have all repeatedly confirmed these same results: rewards undermine performance except for the most trivial or mindless of tasks—and even then, they only increase *quantitative* performance, not qualitative performance.

As Alfie Kohn, lecturer, independent scholar, and bestselling author of *Punished by Rewards*, summarized,

> People who are offered rewards choose easier tasks, are less efficient in using the information available to solve novel problems, and tend to be answer oriented and more illogical in their problem-solving strategies. They seem to work harder and produce more activity, but the activity is of a lower quality, contains more errors, and is more stereotyped and less creative than the work of comparable non-rewarded subjects working on the same problems.[21]

These results, repeatedly produced over the last seventy-five years, have upended the field of behavioral psychology and led to a natural question: When incentivized with rewards and punishments, our performance suffers—but why?

There are many different theories for explaining this phenomenon, but some of the most promising insights have come from understanding the impact that rewards have on our intrinsic motivation. Now, to be clear, being interested and self-motivated to do something won't *guarantee* a quality result—but all things considered, it is at the very least a significant *predictor* of it. As Kohn points out, "Intrinsically motivated people . . . pursue optimal challenges, display greater innovativeness, and tend to perform better under challenging conditions."[22]

That probably isn't surprising. What is surprising is how easily intrinsic motivation is attenuated, even destroyed, when subjected to extrinsic motivators. A good deal of research over the past half-century has explored how extrinsic motivators affect our interests in activities. Here's two well-known studies that helped begin this whole line of investigation.

In 1971, researchers placed adults individually into a waiting room and offered them spatial puzzles to solve. Some participants were offered a monetary reward for solving a puzzle while others were not. After completing a puzzle, they were told to wait in the room until the next and "primary" phase of the psychological study began.

In fact, there was no "next phase"—that was just a ruse. The researchers were really interested in what participants would do given this free time. They discovered that those offered rewards for solving puzzles showed little to no interest in the puzzles during their free time, instead preferring to read magazines or simply daydream. Those not offered monetary rewards, however, continued to solve puzzles during their free time, apparently enjoying the challenge the puzzles presented.

As the principle investigator behind this study would later conjecture, "Money may work to 'buy off' one's intrinsic motivation for an activity."[23] Indeed, this is what later experiments and studies have confirmed. When an activity that we are self-motivated to pursue becomes coerced through incentives and disincentives, our interest in the activity dissipates in response.[24]

Around the same time, a psychologist and researcher was investigating the effects that the Head Start national education program was having on America's children. As part of this program, classrooms were given learning games in the hopes that children would learn more if they could have fun while doing it. In some classrooms, teachers used the games as part of the curriculum and rewarded students with praise, gold-stars, and good grades for utilizing the games, just as they rewarded them for successfully engaging with any other assigned school activity.[25]

In other classrooms, the teachers did not use the games as part of the curriculum and instead simply added them to the pile of toys and materials that students could use during free play. What the psychologist discovered is that in the classrooms where the teachers coerced use of the games through rewards like good grades and gold stars, the children showed no interest in playing the games during their free time. However, in the classrooms where kids were simply offered the chance to play them during free play, they couldn't get enough of these games.[26]

Children, as it turns out, were displaying the same behavior as adults in the study above. Like the adults who lost intrinsic interest in puzzles when offered rewards in exchange for solving them, children lost interest in games when they were offered good grades, gold stars, and praise in exchange for playing them.

The basic conclusion of this research is that extrinsic motivators attenuate, or even destroy, intrinsic motivation. This is why Theory X is a self-fulfilling prophecy. Workers will indeed begin to cross their arms in defiance and sit on their hands unless forced to work *if* they are subjected to a coercive environment. When managers dangle monetary carrots in front of them for doing what they are told, and when they whip workers with disincentives like negative evaluations, performance improvement plans, pay cuts, etc., they create an environment in which workers lose their intrinsic motivation to create, make, and learn. By believing in the myth of necessity, managers and owners have made that myth a reality.

The Myth of Objectivity

The second myth of managerial compensation control is *the myth of objectivity*. Managers would like to believe that their judgements are fair and equitable. That those they reward with raises and promotions truly deserve it and have earned it on the basis of their own merit. They would also like to believe that those they punish deserve it as well, on the basis of their poor performance or misbehavior.

Of course, objective facts do exist, and managerial judgements, both positive and negative, can sometimes reflect truth. Sometimes people truly are terrible at their jobs in ways that everyone can recognize, just as sometimes we encounter people who excel at their job to such an extent that we all simultaneously feel an uneasy mix of awe, admiration, intimidation, and inadequacy within their presence.

But the idea that, on the whole, our modern methods of compensation adjustment are based on clear and unbiased truths about the workforces they are inflicted upon is nothing more than a myth. It's a fairy tale designed to convince workers of the validity of the results and to comfort managers who are forced to make "hard decisions."

This myth is made possible because of often misunderstood aspects of cognitive psychology, the field of psychology that studies perception and reasoning. Most people have an almost unfathomable belief in the validity of their observations, judgements, and decisions. They will confidently declare their foolproof ability to "call it like they see it." Yet the findings of cognitive psychologists make clear that this belief is woefully unfounded. Human perception is selective, at best, and more often than not distorted and warped by our preexisting beliefs and opinions. And human judgements are even worse, based on an unholy alchemy of biases, heuristics, memories, and feelings.

Once again, the goal of this book is not to give you an in-depth understanding of this field of research. There are fantastic books out there already that can do just that, written by experts in cognitive psychology specifically for lay people like us. That being said, I would be remiss not to give you a small tease of some of the fascinating and humbling results of this world of research, so let's look at three illustrative studies.

Study #1: Expectations Warp Perception

Most people take pride in their ability to "call a spade a spade." If someone flashed a playing card at you for half a second, would you be able to tell the suit of the card? If it was a spade, heart, diamond, or club? What about the number on the card? Or the color? Most people would say yes.

Yet, as illustrated by one of the most famous early studies in cognitive psychology, Jerome Bruner and Leo Postman's 1949 paper "On the Perception of Incongruity: A Paradigm,"[27] when people are shown cards that don't match their preexisting expectations—like when they are shown a four of hearts but the heart is black, not red—they struggle to accurately state what's on the card. Some will insist that the card is red, not black. Others correctly report the color as black but insist that the card is a spade or a club, not a heart. Still others struggle to say what they saw; they'll get emotional and say that there was something wrong with the card, that they couldn't make out what it was.[28]

This finding that has been repeatedly confirmed by experiments in cognitive psychology as: "your perceptions are heavily influenced by what you expect to see."[29]

Study #2: The Salience Effect

Imagine two people, we'll call them Al and Bill, are sitting face to face, having a conversation. Next, imagine you're situated behind Al. You can see Bill's face but only the back of Al's head. After the conversation ends, you're asked who was dominating the conversation. Almost without fail you would say Bill—the person whose face you could see. Had you been sitting on the other side, so you could see Al's face and not Bill's, you would almost assuredly have been convinced that Al dominated the conversation.

This example recreates a well-known study from experimental psychologists Shelley Taylor and Susan Fiske.[30] It illustrates a cognitive bias known as "salience effect"[31]—your judgments about a situation are highly affected by what was salient, or stood out to you, in the situation. Your vantage point can affect your judgement by enhancing the salience of a particular element within your field of perception.

But vantage point is only one way to distort perception. As Scott Plous summarizes in his work *The Psychology of Judgement and Decision Making,*

> Additional studies have manipulated the salience of observed people in other ways—by having them wear a boldly patterned shirt

as opposed to a grey shirt, by having them rock in a rocking chair instead of sitting motionless, or by having them sit under a bright light versus a dim light—and the results have tended to be the same. Salient people are perceived as relatively causal."[32]

Even (and rather unsurprisingly) the color of one's skin can trigger the salience effect. In a study in which a group of six actors (three white, three black) carried on a scripted conversation in front of multiple audiences, the audience's judgments about one black actor increased whenever the other two actors were replaced by white actors. In other words, "the very same person saying the very same thing was perceived as talking more and being more influential when he was the only black [person] in the group."[33]

What's important to understand is that this isn't an individual foible or bias—it's a collective phenomenon. Different people of different races, ages, and genders generally experience the same kinds of distortions in perception when presented with the same salience—even though that salience may have absolutely nothing to do with the situation at hand.

Study #3: The Anchoring Bias

Imagine you're a manager who has just been given a stack of peer evaluations for a new employee who reports to you and whom you have yet to get to know. Unbeknownst to you, the stack has been ordered. On the top is a very positive peer review with scores of "10 out of 10" for performance, collaboration, and creativity.

On the bottom is a very negative review that presents your employee with scores of "1 out of 10" in the same categories. In between are middle-of-the-road reviews that are neither especially positive nor negative. What conclusion would you draw about your employee after working through the stack?

If the stack is ordered as I described, then you would almost certainly give your employee a *positive* performance evaluation because that first, very positive, review would *anchor* all of your further impressions. However, had the stack simply been sorted in the opposite order, so that the very negative review was on top while the very positive review was on bottom, you would have almost certainly given your employee a negative performance evaluation—again, because that first, very negative, review would have anchored all of your further impressions.

Your judgements about others are anchored by first impressions and will always struggle to deviate too far from that initial impression. This is known as the *anchoring* effect—a cognitive bias that has been demonstrated in dozens of studies.

For example, when the Nobel Prize–winning psychologist and economist Daniel Kahneman asked people, "Is the percentage of African countries in the United Nations greater or less than <X>%?" and then followed that with "What is the exact percentage of African countries in the United Nations," he found that people's answers were significantly influenced by "X" (i.e., by the percentage he used in the first question). If he used a percentage of "10%" in the first question, he found that responses to the second question would result in a relatively low median estimate of 25%. But if he used "65%" in the first question, the median response to the second question would rise to "45%."[34]

The results of this study have been replicated dozens of times since then by other cognitive psychologists. Regardless of whether people are estimating the percentage of African nations in the UN, the price of a college textbook, or the likelihood of a nuclear war, their estimates are *significantly* biased, or anchored, by initial values presented to them.

As Plous explains, "The effects of anchoring are pervasive and extremely robust . . . . People adjust insufficiently from anchor values, regardless of whether judgment concerns the chances of nuclear war, the value of a house, or any number of other topics."[35] What's more, "it is difficult to protect against the effects of anchoring, partly because incentives for accuracy seldom work, and partly because the anchor values themselves often go unnoticed."[36]

These are just a handful of humbling and unsettling examples about the psychology of perception, judgement, and decision-making. The last half-century of results in cognitive psychology lay bare the myth of objectivity for what it is: a myth and nothing more. Our perceptions, judgments, and reasoning have little to do with objective facts—and much to do with subjective beliefs. Which is why performance evaluations are an exercise in subjectivity and bias. They are—*at best*—an unconscious mix of assumptions, predictions, feelings, heuristics, and memories. In aggregate, they tell us much more about the managers than the managed.

Before we move on, please know that although the words in this section may sound harsh and unforgiving, I believe we should have empathy and compassion for everyone (including ourselves) caught up in coercive systems of managerial compensation control. I have been on all sides of it. I have been on the receiving end of biased, one-sided managerial judgements that have affected my life and the lives of those I love and care for.

But I have also been on the giving end—as a manager forced to make "hard decisions." I have believed in the myths of necessity and objectivity because being caught up in this system of domination and coercion is almost too much to bear without the comfort that the myths provide.

This system hurts *everyone* involved—it diminishes the humanity in both the dominators and the dominated. But thankfully there is a better way. Radically collaborative organizations all over the world are experimenting with devolved systems of compensation management. Let's turn to those systems now.

Exploring the Alternatives

We've already looked at one example of how to devolve pay into a radically collaborative organization. In the last chapter, I began with an overview of what is, to my knowledge, the most radically devolved organization on the planet: Matt Black Systems. As part of that overview, I snuck in a basic sketch of their devolved compensation system. Under their fractal organizational model, every employee is a virtual company of one, which, as we saw, devolves managerial responsibilities and administrative duties down to the individual. But as we also saw, the fractal model at Matt Black Systems devolves pay too.

Every employee at Matt Black Systems owns a personal profit-and-loss account, which makes clear the revenue they generate, the expenses they incur, and the surplus (if any) they achieve. Their take-home pay is a function of that surplus. Although every employee commits to a base wage—i.e., a wage that they believe they will "pay for" with their labors—their real earnings come as a percentage of the monthly profit they generate. Twenty percent of their monthly surplus goes directly into their pockets as a bonus, which, for many employees, not only doubles or triples their base pay but sets their total pay far above their industry average.

Although Matt Black Systems is a small manufacturing organization, the basic idea behind their devolved pay process has proven to scale to a significant size. In the introduction to this book, I used Haier—the massive, eighty-thousand-person innovation and manufacturing organization—as an existence proof for the viability of radical collaboration. As we saw, Haier is broken into thousands of small microenterprises, each averaging around ten to fifteen employees. These microenterprises freely contract with each other for goods and services, and taken together, they form a self-organizing swarm of radically collaborative teams.

Well, it turns out that pay for colleagues within each microenterprise is devolved in much the same way as pay at Matt Black Systems. Although everyone in the microenterprise begins with a low base rate of pay, they increase their take home pay by achieving "leading targets" they set for their microenterprise. Leading targets run the gamut from revenue growth to cost cutting to the extent of user-involvement in the product design process, and they are set at levels that are audacious, to say the least.

For example, microenterprises at Haier tend to set revenue growth targets that are four to ten times higher than the industry average.[37] Although that may sound daunting, even grueling, to some, keep in mind that not only do microenterprises routinely hit their leading targets, they do so by creating a culture of continuous transformation and innovation.

As Gary Hamel and Dr. Michele Zanini, the world-renowned organizational theorists and coauthors of *Humanocracy*, put it, "Leading targets compel microenterprises to continually reexamine their core assumptions. As in a startup, everyone knows that more of the same won't cut it."[38] By aspiring to unprecedented levels of growth—and by basing individual pay on that collective achievement—Haier has inspired new levels of imagination and creativity in everyone's day-to-day work.

There are lots of fascinating nuances and sophistications to the pay system at Haier that you can read more about in books like *Humanocracy*. But the sum of it is this: Haier has devolved the control of pay out of the hands of managers and down to individuals by directly connecting an individual's salary to the value that they and their microenterprise generate for customers. As Zhang Ruimin, Haier's CEO, summed up, "At Haier we are no longer paying our employees. Instead, they are paid by customers."[39]

One interesting facet of both Matt Black's and Haier's devolved pay systems involves investment and innovation. At Matt Black Systems, for example, a fifth of an individual's monthly profit goes into a personal investment account that they are free to use at their discretion. They could purchase new instruments, tools, or machinery either by themselves or by pooling their investment money with others. Or they could use the money to invest in new business opportunities and speculative ventures.

As Matt Black's founders put it, "The individual is the sole steward of this liquid asset. Our aim is to nurture the entrepreneurial talents of our people, not only their productivity. Many people have tens of thousands of pounds accrued in their investment accounts; company money that they are the sole steward of."[40]

The individual stewardship of corporate profit is a way to further devolve managerial control and further increase both individual and collective autonomy over the work and the workplace.

Haier has also devolved investment into the organization—and beyond—through a "zero-fund" entrepreneurial support program that, in effect, means that new ventures in the organization are initially self-funded by employees, by external investors, by potential customers, or by all three.[41]

For example, would-be entrepreneurs at Haier are often some of the first investors in their microenterprise—which can lead to a significant windfall. Remember ThundeRobot, the microenterprise for quality gaming laptops? By pooling individual earnings, the employees behind the new venture invested enough money near the outset to secure a 20% stake in ThundeRobot.[42] Considering the fact that ThundeRobot is now valued at over $300 million US,[43] that stake has led to some significant returns for employees who, in any other company, would never have had the opportunity or means to create an internal startup.

Haier's customer-centered approach to product design has also led to another common form of investment: crowdfunding. The majority of incubating microenterprises at Haier are, at least in part, crowdfunded ventures in which would-be customers fund design and development in exchange for helping set the product direction and for access to early-release prototypes and betas.[44] Not only does this offset Haier's own investment risks, but it also creates clear signals for market demand and product viability.

The end result of Haier's investment strategy is a culture of innovation and entrepreneurship that has more in common with Silicon Valley than Wall Street. As Zhang summarized to the authors of the book *Corporate Rebels*, at Haier, "Everyone can be their own CEO."[45]

Although Matt Black Systems and Haier have found success with their methods of compensation devolution, these aren't the only ways to devolve pay. There are two other approaches that are quickly gaining traction around the world: the *Deming Pay System* and *self-managed salary*.

The Deming Pay System

The Deming Pay System is named after W. Edwards Deming, who many readers will recognize as the forefather of Lean Manufacturing. Deming did not mince words when it came to the managerial control of compensation. He called it the "destroyer of people."[46] He said that instead of motivating people to do their best, "Everyone propels himself forward, or tries to, for his own good, on his own life preserver. The organization is the loser."[47] He told his readers and clients to "abolish incentive pay and pay based on performance," because only then would they "give everyone a chance to take pride in [their] work."[48]

Although Deming's research was founded early on in systems thinking and statistical variation, many of his insights into human motivation presaged the field of cognitive science. In his work and writings, Deming advocated for a system of compensation divorced from coercive management techniques. As one of Deming's colleagues related,

> Deming would pay every employee—right up through the chief executive—a straight salary or wages. Those in the same job would be paid roughly the same; some differences would be created by seniority, since everyone would get annual raises. Those raises would be uniform not based on merit. . . . The one acceptable bonus plan to Deming is profit sharing. But every employee would get an equal share. The chief executive getting the same bonus as a factory worker? "Well, why not? Certainly," says Deming, looking astonished by the question.[49]

This recommendation is simple yet radical. It's also radically different from the approach pioneered by Matt Black Systems and Haier. Instead of connecting each individual's pay to their individual contribution within the system, the Deming Pay System attempts to eliminate any individual connection at all.

AT A GLANCE

Viisi: Fintech company focused on mortgage advice. Employs forty people. Based in the Netherlands. Notable for implementing the Deming Pay System.

Viisi, a Holacracy-powered fintech company in the Netherlands, is an example of the Deming Pay System in the wild. At Viisi, everyone in the same role is on the same pay curve, which itself is based on industry benchmarks and pegged at the top quartile of industry salary ranges. Annual raises are automatic and uniform for everyone in the same role—and since the pay curves are mapped out for thirty-five years into the future, every-one knows exactly what they will make in the coming years.

Additionally, individual bonuses are banned at Viisi, out of concern that they would diminish intrinsic motivation. The founders of Viisi want to ensure that people pursue roles based on personal passions, not mone-tary incentives like bonuses.

Viisi's model was at least partially inspired by the results from the field of motivation theory and cognitive science that we explored earlier. As Viisi's founder stated,

> Many will be familiar with Daniel Kahneman's research or Daniel Pink's videos, which show that rewarding more work not only doesn't work but is actually counterproductive. . . . Most companies ignore this and still work with the carrot. But this counteracts team-work. On the other hand, if all the haggling and bonus payments are dropped, it promotes collegiality and intrinsic motivation.[50]

Like Deming, Viisi's founders see managerial compensation control as not just ineffective but actively destructive. They have devolved compen-sation in order to remove coercion from the process and to eliminate an individual's day-to-day hopes and fears about how their individual work might or might not affect their pay.

As we'll see in the following chapter, this is not only a way to create an environment in which intrinsic motivation can freely flower, it's also a way to gratify a range of higher-level human needs, including security and trust. By making salary transparent and raises automatic and uniform, the Deming Pay System eliminates feelings of instability that coercive pay pro-cesses engender while communicating a sense of individual and collective trust.

Self-Managed Salary

The last and final system of devolved compensation we'll look at in this chapter is self-managed salary. The idea is as simple as it sounds: individu-als manage their own salary. They decide what they make and they revisit that decision whenever they want. If they feel like they should have a raise, they give themselves a raise.

Among all of the devolved systems of compensation, this one con-tradicts the tenets of Theory X more than any other. If employees are inherently lazy and unmotivated—if they will cross their arms and refuse to work without externally controlled monetary incentives—then there is no way in the world that self-managed salaries could ever work. Workers would milk the company for all its worth without ever lifting a finger.

As we already know, Theory X has been shown to be less than true, to say the least. In reality, self-managed pay works. Let's see how.

AT A GLANCE

GrantTree: Helps organizations acquire government R&D grants. Employs sixty-five people. Founded in 2010. Based in London. Notable for pioneering self-managed pay.

Consider GrantTree, a UK-based company that helps businesses secure government research grants. Colleagues there use the advice process to self-manage their pay. They look at factors like industry averages, time in role, personal growth and experience, and the financial situation of the company. They then put a proposal in front of a panel of peers and ask for their advice.

To be clear, this panel has no authority over the employee's decision. As one employee there explains, "Colleagues are not there to say yes or no or to approve it. They are there to ask questions and give you some feedback."[51] When an employee seeks advice for a salary increase, they are free to take the advice or leave it; the decision, at the end of the day, is their responsibility.

AT A GLANCE

Pod Group: Enterprise network operator (ENO) for Internet of Things. Twenty-five employees. Based in San Francisco. Founded 1999. Notable for self-managing culture and self-managed pay.

Pod Group, a radically collaborative technology company that specializes in artificial intelligence and Internet of Things devices, has also transitioned to self-managed pay. They initially wanted to pursue a version of the Deming Pay System, where someone's salary would be automatically derived from a formula. The formula would include things like a general benchmark for the technology sector with multipliers for cost of living, role, and years of experience.

However, they struggled to come up with a formula that would fairly compensate people, given that people live in different places, have different goals, and exhibit different needs during different phases of their lives. So, they threw out the formulas altogether and decided to trust people to fairly self-manage their own salaries through the advice process. When an employee wants to change their salary at Pod Group, they present their compensation change proposal to a panel of peers. Those peers give them feedback—but, like GrantTree, the final decision is left to the employee.

With all salaries transparent and with peer groups giving each other feedback on compensation adjustments, the employees at Pod Group have self-managed compensation without bringing financial ruin upon the company, as Theory X would predict. As their CEO explains,

> Employees are aware that the level of positive recognition from each of their colleagues will also take into account the salary earned. If colleagues think you are earning too much money, there is a very real danger that your interaction with them will change. As most people value peer camaraderie, they don't want to appear greedy in the eyes of their colleagues.[52]

Since implementing self-managed pay in 2017, Pod Group has seen salaries rise around 10% above their previous level. However, they have also seen their retention rate skyrocket at the same time. Since the recruiting and training cost of replacing an employee that quits is conservatively estimated at twice that of the employee's annual pay,[53] the 10% increase in salaries has been more than offset by the increase in retention. If anything, Pod Group is saving money.

Conclusion

I began this chapter with a bold claim: the managerial control of compensation is a coercive calamity, both for organizations and individuals. It is a process full of bias, based on myths, and has counterintuitive and counterproductive effects on motivation and productivity. It is at the root of domination and coercion within hierarchical organizations. It must be devolved for the sake of individual well-being and collective success.

I would now like to end this chapter with a personal appeal. If you are a leader in a traditional company—either for a division of the company or for the company as a whole—then please, take that first step toward the devolution of compensation. You don't have to work out all the details up front. You don't even have to have a specific plan for how to do it. But you have to start the conversation. As much as I wish they could, your employees can't take that first step for you. By definition, they don't have the power to change compensation. They are structurally confined to a system of coercion and domination. And they are disincentivized from even mentioning the idea to you.

The fractal model, the Deming Pay System, and self-managed pay are three predominant methods of compensation devolution. But they're not the only ways to do it. The specific mechanics of the devolved compensation system matter far less than the intent. Eliminate coercion and bias. Increase individual agency and collective trust. Preserve and nurture intrinsic motivation, that most powerful and most fragile of human gifts. These are the outcomes that matter. Together, you and your employees can work out the details.

Questions for Reflection:

» Which method of devolved compensation most appeals to you personally? The fractal model, in which your pay is a function of the surplus you generate? The Deming Pay System, in which everyone has set salaries and set raises? Or self-managed pay, in which everyone chooses their own salaries and their own raises with openness and transparency?

» Which of these devolved compensation methods do you think makes the most sense for your organization?

» Which devolved compensation method do you think would be easiest to transition to for your organization? Which would be the hardest? Why?

CHAPTER 5

IMPERATIVE #3: DEFICIENCY GRATIFICATION

A little over three years into his first tour of duty as an engineer at CivicActions, Andy Hawks left for a similar consulting organization one of his good friends had recently joined. This organization specialized in an open-source technology stack that Hawks was an expert in. It was filled with intelligent and talented people that Hawks admired. The projects were many and varied, so Hawks would never fear growing bored. And he enjoyed a good salary with equally good benefits. On paper, this organization had everything he needed. In practice, something was missing.

When he began to compare his experiences at this new organization to his experiences at CivicActions, a word came to mind: "ego-driven." The workplace culture at this new organization engendered ego-driven behavior. The intelligence and talents of the employees were not just a means to problem-solving and value creation—they were also a means to one-upsmanship and politicking. It was an environment brimming with intelligence yet lacking in empathy. Over time, it began to wear Hawks down, but it also helped Hawks put into words what it was that had made CivicActions such a special experience for him.

He felt that, unlike at this new organization, CivicActions had created a culture of "empathy and appreciation," as he related to me in our interviews. In both casual and structured interactions, people had routinely and habitually "treated each other as human beings," empathizing with each other's experiences and respecting and even honoring each other's perspectives. At CivicActions, he experienced a sense of connection and belonging that, in his words, enabled not just him, but "*everyone* to do better work." He longed to return to an environment like that—so that's exactly what he did. He left the new organization and returned to CivicActions, where his colleagues welcomed him back with open arms.

Although Hawks didn't know it at the time, CivicActions was, for him, a *deficiency-gratifying* environment—a technical term from the field of positive psychology that we will explore throughout this chapter.

While the details are rich and deep, the basic idea is simple to understand: a deficiency-gratifying environment is one in which people mutually satisfy each other's higher-level human needs, like security, trust, esteem, and respect. Hawks returned to CivicActions because the colleagues there replenished a range of needs that his experiences in the other organization had rendered deficient. He didn't just need the right tech stack or varied projects or intelligent and talented peers. He needed to feel trusted by his collaborators and secure in his working relationships. He needed to feel a sense of belonging and connection with those he worked with in order to find meaning and fulfillment in his work—which is exactly what CivicActions provided.

In this respect, CivicActions is not unique. Each of our pioneers has created deficiency-gratifying environments—in which radical collaborators freely fulfill each other's higher level human needs and thereby create a foundation for meaning, purpose, and fulfillment.

Deficiency Gratification

Readers are undoubtedly familiar with the concept of physiological deficiencies. A vitamin C deficiency, for example, leads to a condition known as "scurvy"—the one-time scourge of the British Navy. Women, and pregnant women in particular, are no stranger to anemia, resulting from iron deficiencies. And many vegetarians are familiar with the lethargy resulting from a protein deficiency.

Our bodies have certain physiological needs. Without them, our health declines, and we experience the symptoms associated with our deficiency. However, the cure is typically simple: gratify the deficiency. Suffering from scurvy? Eat an orange. Fatigued from an iron deficiency? Down a steak. Weak and tired from a protein deficiency? Boil an egg.

Within the medical world, deficiency illnesses and gratification cures have been understood since the 1750s. Psychological deficiency illnesses, however, are a more recent discovery. Abraham Maslow, a mid-twentieth-century psychologist, was among the first to explore them. He's one of the founders of the field of positive psychology, the study of mental well-being, which stands in contrast to clinical psychology, the study of mental illness.

Maslow articulated that the process of deficiency motivation and gratification applies not just to our physical health but to our mental health as well. Humans have a number of higher-level, psychological needs—like security, trust, and esteem—that work in much the same way as our lower-level physiological needs. When deprived of higher-level psychological needs, our mental health suffers, but we also become motivated to rectify our deficiencies. We will be naturally, instinctively drawn to deficiency-gratifying environments. And under free-choice conditions, we will engage in those environments in quantities sufficient to remedy our mental health.[1]

As Maslow summarized in his seminal work, *Toward a Psychology of Being* (bold added for emphasis):

> The human being has, as part of his intrinsic construction, not only physiological needs but also truly psychological ones. They may be considered as **deficiencies** which must be optimally fulfilled by the **environment** in order to avoid sickness and subjective ill-being. They can be called basic, or biological, and likened to the need for salt or calcium or vitamin D because—
>
> a) The deprived person yearns for their **gratification** persistently.
> b) Their deprivation makes the person sicken and wither.
> c) Gratifying them is therapeutic, curing the deficiency-illness.
> d) Steady supplies forestall these illnesses.
> e) Healthy (gratified) people do not demonstrate these deficiencies.[2]

The field of positive psychology has articulated a number of higher-level human needs that all humans exhibit, several of which we've already explored in this book:

- **Autonomy:** Our need to control our own lives and lived experiences—to manage ourselves without the interference or domination of others; to decide from moment to moment and day-to-day what commitments we make and how we will go about honoring them.
- **Fairness:** Our need to relate to others on the basis of equality and to not be disadvantaged by favoritism, discrimination, or domination.

- **Security:** Our need for a sense of stability and predictability in our lives—to feel like we can go about our day without the worry that someone or something is working against us, waiting to yank the rug out from under us.
- **Esteem:** Our need to feel good about who we are and what we are capable of—and our need to feel like those around us hold us in that same high regard.
- **Trust:** Our need for others to believe in us as we follow our instincts and take risks—to support us, even when, and especially when, we fail.
- **Meaning:** Our need to feel like what we do matters; that it enhances our lives and the lives of those around us; that we are part of and inseparable from that grand adventure that is the human spirit.
- **Love:** Our need to hold someone so dear that we are willing to sacrifice for them—and our need for someone else to hold us in that same regard.

These are all human needs. We don't just need food, water, shelter, and air. We need security, autonomy, fairness, esteem, trust, meaning, and love. Provided these needs, we thrive; deprived of these needs, we wither.

One important thing to note about all of these needs is that they can only be satisfied by others. For example, we can't feel secure or autonomous in our lives without at least some cooperation from those around us. Similarly, self-esteem is as much a function of our own self-image as it is a function of the regard of others. Love, trust, fairness, even meaning, are all intertwined with our fellow human beings. We depend on others for wholeness in our lives—just as they depend on us.

As Maslow wrote, "Just as trees need sun, water, and food from the environment, so do all people need safety, love and status from their environment . . . . The needs for safety, belongingness, love relations and for respect can be satisfied only by other people, i.e., only from outside the person. This means considerable dependence on the environment."[3]

In this sense, deficiency gratification is the gift that we give to each other. We can, one on one, gratify each other's human needs by helping each other to feel security, autonomy, esteem, and belongingness. But we can also create organizational environments and cultures that enable the repeated and systematic gratification of deficiency needs.

As noted in Chapter 1, this isn't just an ethical imperative—it's a business booster. As global studies like the *HOW Report* illustrate, financially competitive outcomes are tightly correlated with the health and well-being of the organization's members. An organization simply can't thrive so long as its members wither under growth-inhibiting conditions. In order to sustain a competitive edge in the marketplace, organizations must figure out how to create a deficiency-gratifying environment. Let's see now how our radically collaborative pioneers have done just that.

Pioneering Practices for Deficiency Gratification

Each of our pioneers developed a number of deficiency-gratifying practices, ranging in duration, impact, and frequency. Individually, these practices gratify one or more of our higher-level human needs; collectively, they generate a workplace culture in which people can show up for each other as full, unguarded, vulnerable human beings. We'll start with small yet frequent deficiency-gratifying practices that can be incorporated into daily interactions, and we'll end with large yet infrequent practices that exemplify and reinforce an overall paradigm of psychological health.

Balance Scores

Among the simplest of our pioneers' deficiency-gratifying practices is *balance scores*—a technique CivicActions created several years ago and which it utilizes in meetings every day. A balance score is a number between one and ten that "briefly communicates how you are doing at knowing your priorities and honoring those priorities" along three specific dimensions: personal (e.g., personal relationships, mental and physical health), professional (career goals, skills growth, etc.) and spiritual (a definition left to the individual but meant to encompass a sense of higher purpose).[4] The score is entirely subjective and the ultimate meaning of "balance" is left up to each individual.

Colleagues at CivicActions begin each meeting by sharing their balance score with everyone. Someone who gives a ten, for example, would probably feel completely present in the moment. They would be in the meeting because they want to be in the meeting—because it perfectly aligns with their intrinsic motivation at that time. There would be no distractions weighing on their mind. Their thoughts would be fully focused on the present, instead of being distracted by some stress in the past or some worry about the future. Clearly, a ten is a high bar that most would struggle to achieve. But thankfully, that's not the point. Balance scores are not a way to gamify your life but to share with others your humanity.

Aaron Pava, the cofounder of CivicActions, said in our interview that his typical baseline score is an eight—which other people with whom he regularly meets with have noticed. So when he shares a balance score significantly below eight, he's signaling to others that he is struggling to feel whole and balanced in that moment.

Balance scores are intentionally presented without comment so you can share your score without fear that others will immediately press for intimate details. However, there's nothing stopping someone who cares about you from reaching out to you later and asking how you're doing. Which is, in fact, what often happens.

As Pava noted in our interview, "When I share a score below my baseline, people reach out to me and ask me how I'm doing. I have hundreds of examples of people encouraging me to step away for an hour and take a walk, do some yoga, or meditate. We've created a culture of care because we're communicating our balance to each other."

In our interview, Andy Hawks reported a similar experience when he shares balance scores that are lower than his baseline: "My baseline is a seven—so if I check in at five, people will send me direct messages like 'Hey, are you doing OK?' or 'What can I do to support you?' or 'Reach out to me if there's anything you need.'"

By openly sharing their sense of balance with each other every day, colleagues at CivicActions feel a greater sense of connectedness with each other.

Both Pava and Hawks used the same word to characterize the type of environment that practices like balance scores create: trust. Balance scores help gratify our need for trust because they create an environment in which we are trusted to share more of ourselves. Trust gratification is not only a boon for mental health—it's a booster for organizational productivity.

As we noted in Chapter 1, "trust" is one of the key differentiators between radically collaborative organizations and traditional organizations. According to the *HOW Report*, the high levels of trust found in radically collaborative organizations lead to thirty-two times the amount of risk-taking as their hierarchical peers. That risk-taking, in turn, results in eleven times the amount of innovation and six times the amount of performance.[5]

Balance scores are an exercise in trust building with powerful downstream effects on organizational efficacy—and some of our other pioneers have adopted similar practices.

Check-Ins

In Holacracy, there's a close analog to balance scores called the check-in. At the beginning of every governance meeting, Holacracy circles go around the room and give everyone the space to check in by sharing something that's weighing on their minds and tugging at their attention.

Vanessa Slavich, one of the founding partners at cLabs, has sometimes used this moment to share details about her physical and emotional state as she has struggled with a rare and hard-to-treat disease. A sick family member, domestic strife, and corporate time pressures are also examples of things people share.

The belief behind this practice is that when we openly name whatever factors are weighing on us in the moment, we reduce the power that those factors hold over us—that we become more "present and focused," in the words of Brian J. Robertson, Holacracy's founder.[6] By checking in, we also invite understanding, since sharing our mental states and the factors behind them makes it possible for others to adjust to us and to empathize with us.

It's interesting that, like balance scores, check-ins are to be presented without comment. In order to open up to others and share intimate details about mental and physical states, people have to feel like they can do so without judgement or prying. The goal is to be heard and seen, not analyzed and fixed.

Robertson refers to the check-in as a "sacred space" that must be protected from cross-talk, advice, and even words of sympathy.[7] Only then will people let their guard down and speak freely because only then will they feel trusted to share with others their whole self.

It's not the words of others, in this case, that gratify our deficiencies—it's the attention. When others give us their full attention, they create a circle of security and trust that helps us open up and share more about who we are. We'll look again at the openness engendered by this practice in the next chapter.

Meeting Prompts

Balance scores and check-ins are a way to help others connect with our thoughts and feelings in the moment. But, of course, we are all more than our present thoughts and feelings. We are a menagerie of past experiences and a repository of future aspirations. Our words and deeds in the present enfold that vast context—and a big part of trusting someone is seeing them within that broader horizon. That's why our pioneers have embraced a number of practices that help people connect along all of those dimensions.

Several teams at Nearsoft, for example, begin their meetings with a prompt unrelated to the meeting's topic, designed to bring joy into the meeting while helping the participants gain a deeper connection with each other.

In our interview, Nyx Zamora expressed her surprise by how much she learned about her peers when they used the prompt, "What job would you have had if you had lived in medieval times?" When a group of elite software makers are forced to imagine life without electricity, they have to reflect on what it is about modern technology that really kindles their interest and passion.

The answers, according to Zamora, were a surprising mixture of hilarity and depth that you would not expect from a question so seemingly benign—and Zamora ended the session with a deeper sense of connection to her teammates.

cLabbers often start their tactical Holacracy meetings with similar prompts. Pranay Mohan, a product manager at cLabs, recounted to me an especially memorable prompt along with the exchange that ensued.

> A member of our product circle asked everyone to share one physical item that they owned that was personally meaningful to them. Although the meeting was over a video conference, the intensity was palpable. People really bared their soul in a way that is uncommon in traditional corporate structures where you're actually disincentivized from being vulnerable.

Moments like these are a daily experience at many of our pioneers, yielding dividends for individual well-being and organizational efficacy. But to a revenue-obsessed leader, they can seem like a waste of time since it may not be clear how any specific experience improves the bottom line.

It's important to see these practices as a necessary investment—which is exactly how CivicActions has come to defend them.

Pod Groups

As a reminder, CivicActions is a consulting organization in which consultants bill clients by the hour. So when they take time away from client work, they very clearly and directly reduce revenue. With such a tangible revenue metric, it is important for an organization like CivicActions to underscore the long-term value of deficiency-gratifying practices—since many of those practices may not be billable.

In addition to balance scores, the colleagues at CivicActions have collectively organized a nonbillable, deficiency-gratifying practice called *pod groups*. These are self-organizing groups of colleagues, each consisting of around fifteen people, and each with an entirely social mission. Their goal is to connect with each other, get to know each other, and have fun together. Each pod group meets weekly for thirty minutes to an hour—but the format is entirely self-organized. Some pods have developed a pattern of facilitators and prompts to elicit interesting conversations, while others have a more free-flowing, unstructured approach.

Despite the diversity of cultures between the various pod groups, the deficiency-gratifying goal is the same: develop the bonds of fellowship between each other that make radical collaboration possible. Aaron Pava explained in our interview,

> I'm sure that if you added up all the time we've spent in social groups, like pod calls, instead of billing clients the number would be quite significant. If you're running a business and driving only toward efficiency, you might object to these practices. But for us, it's not even a question because it's these social connections and the trust that's built up through them that make the space and the flow.

Andy Hawks elaborated, "Not only does it create this culture that allows us to be more connected, it also allows better cohesion within the teams and allows us to do better work and just perform better all around because of that culture."

For Pava, Hawks, and all of the other colleagues at CivicActions, the social connections forged in these settings form a foundation of trust—without which there could be no radical collaboration in the first place.

Practices like balance scores, check-ins, and pod groups operate at the level of direct, interpersonal interaction. But that's not the only way to gratify deficiencies. Let's look now at a structural form of deficiency gratification—one that we've already considered near the beginning of this book: autonomy of allocation.

The Deficiency Gratification of Autonomy of Allocation

In Chapter 2, we looked at the organizational impact of autonomy of allocation—in which colleagues choose for themselves what to work on and who to work with. We saw that not only did it leverage the superpower of intrinsic motivation, it also shined a light on troubled projects and interpersonal strife that would, in a dominator hierarchy, have been swept under the rug.

We can now add another lens on which to view autonomy of allocation: it's a structural form of deficiency gratification. When an organization lets makers choose what to work on, they communicate respect for the interests of makers and trust in their ability to wield those interests responsibly. For example, Pranay Mohan's experience with autonomy of allocation at cLabs helped him discover what it was that he was truly passionate about.

As a reminder, Mohan leveraged autonomy of allocation to pursue work with the World Bank Group, a world-renowned NGO. But after joining the effort, he discovered that he had little interest in the slow-moving realities of NGO work and returned to his former work on crypto protocols after a few months.

Whipsaw allocations like this may seem like a short-term economic loss of efficiency, but in the long term, the ability to discover what one is truly passionate about will pay dividends for the organization. It creates high-trust environments in which employees aren't just engaged—they're inspired.

As the researchers behind the *HOW Report* note, "Inspiration is 27% more predictive of performance than employee engagement . . . . When employees are authentically dedicated, deeply accountable, and fully responsible, they contribute in an enduring and consequential way."[8]

In other words, deficiency-gratifying practices and structures are inefficient only when seen from a short-term perspective. In the long term, they are an investment in individual inspiration and organizational performance. For most of the radically collaborative pioneers in this book, that investment is implicit, even metaphorical. At CivicActions, that investment is rendered explicit and literal, thanks to an annual practice known as the Coin Ceremony.

The Coin Ceremony

If you've ever been in the US military, then you have likely heard of, or even received, a "challenge coin." Although challenge coins were originally used to challenge the identity of service members and to root out spies, over time they became a way to recognize troops and individuals for valor and bravery during the course of a special mission. Modern-day challenge coins are often emblazoned with words and insignia significant to the troop. And over the past few decades, nonmilitary government agencies have adopted the practice too. This is how CivicActions first became familiar with the concept. After seeing challenge coins in action through their government consulting work, they adopted and adapted the idea into an annual practice they call the *Coin Ceremony*.

Here's how the Coin Ceremony works. Every year, during their self-organized annual retreat, colleagues take turns presenting each other with custom-made coins and expressing gratitude and appreciation for each other in the process. It's important to note here that they are *not* recognizing each other for the work that they do. Instead, they are explicitly expressing gratitude for the *being* of the other—for who the other is as a person and for what they bring into the world and into each other's lives.

As Aaron Pava said in our interview, "Everything that makes CivicActions special comes down to the Coin Ceremony. The work we do with the government day-to-day is hard. We're often improving or replacing massive government systems that millions of people depend on. Our work can be stressful, even draining, and the Coin Ceremony is a way for us to recharge our emotional and spiritual batteries."

Andy Hawks told me that the intensity of the experience can become too much for him, leading him to break down and cry. "We're just not used to that level of vulnerability, honesty, and appreciation," he explained.

In this sense, the Coin Ceremony is the quintessential deficiency-gratifying practice. It epitomizes a culture of balance and wholeness, in which the gift of deficiency gratification is made visible and literal. It is an outpouring of respect, esteem, security, even love, and it creates the foundation of trust and inspiration from which all radical collaboration builds upon.

Conclusion

Building a culture of deficiency gratification is easy when an organization is small. For example, I'm sure that many readers have experienced an intense sense of shared purpose and connectedness while working closely with others in a startup. That's because when we band together into small, heterarchical groups, deficiency gratification comes naturally to us. The challenge is, how do you maintain that environment as the organization grows?

Most organizations all but eliminate deficiency-gratifying environments as they grow by instituting a dominator hierarchy. But even radically collaborative, heterarchical organizations can struggle to maintain an environment deficiency gratification.

Pranay Mohan of cLabs told me, "Our organizational size has ballooned, and that shared feeling that I got even a year ago has been harder to manage—especially in a remote, pandemic world." However, Mohan remains hopeful that the deficiency-gratifying practices and rituals at cLabs will, in the end, compensate for the challenges of rapid growth. He says that even something as simple as a prompt about the changing of the seasons, from winter to spring, can help them connect with each other, and reflect on their shared humanity.

Of course, at some point, it will become impossible for everyone in an organization to have a deep sense of personal connection to everyone else. But that doesn't mean the organization can't still be a wellspring of deficiency gratification. If Haier, the eighty-thousand-person megacorporation broken up into thousands of microenterprises is any indicator, deficiency gratification and overall size are orthogonal concerns. If you resist the temptation to institute a dominator hierarchy and instead maintain a self-organizing heterarchy of small teams, you can continue to enable everyone to give the gift of gratification.

In this chapter, we looked at two primary benefits of deficiency gratification: individual well-being and organizational performance. However, there is a third benefit that we have yet to consider: the liberation of candor and vulnerability. Deficiency-gratifying environments can liberate everyone's ability to not only be open about who they are but about what they believe and why they believe it. This leads to a mode of collective reasoning known as *candid vulnerability*, and it has some stunning consequences for organizational efficacy that we'll spend the next chapter exploring.

» Look back over the deficiency needs and definitions spelled out earlier in this chapter. Which needs do you feel most gratified in? Which needs call out for gratification in you?

» What activities, structures, or relationships within your workplace gratify your deficiency needs? When do you feel a sense of safety and security, trust and autonomy, esteem and belongingness?

» What activities, structures, or relationships within your workplace threaten your deficiency needs? When do you feel insecure, stressed, manipulated, controlled, disadvantaged, disrespected, displaced?

» Deficiency gratification is a gift that we give to each other. What could you do to give that gift to those around you? How could you increase the sense of security, autonomy, fairness, esteem, trust, belongingness, and love within those who you interact with on a daily basis?

» This chapter details several deficiency-gratifying practices, like balance scores, check-ins, peer pods, and Coin Ceremonies. Which practices would be easiest to introduce to your organization or on your team? Which would be the hardest? Why?

CHAPTER 6

IMPERATIVE #4: CANDID VULNERABILITY

In previous chapters, we've seen how the developers at TIM Group drew inspiration from a number of radically collaborative pioneers, like the Johnsonville Sausage factory, the GE jet-engine factory, and the innovation organization W. L. Gore. Although the stories and practices from these organizations catalyzed the transformation at TIM Group, the developers there soon realized that there was a missing piece to their radically collaborative puzzle. Even though they had scrapped their dominator *hierarchies*, they still found themselves mired in dominator *behaviors*.

Meetings, for example, too often became scenes of conflict rather than collaboration—in which individuals spent more time defending their positions than exploring the alternatives. Similarly, in company-wide forums like town halls, organizational shortcomings were more likely to be hidden and undiscussed than illuminated and openly addressed. So developers at TIM Group were faced with a dilemma: How could they effectively self-manage their organization if dominator hierarchies had shaped their mindset and behaviors? What new ways of thinking and behaving were necessary to move toward a culture of heterarchy and radical collaboration effectively? Once again, they looked to the literature for ideas and inspiration—and once again, they found it.

The developers at TIM Group stumbled into a field of sociology that studies the two predominant reasoning processes that individuals use inside organizations. The first process is known as *Model I: Defensive Reasoning*, in which individuals advocate for their positions while concealing the hidden world of observations, inferences, and assumptions that lead them to their positions in the first place. The second process is known as *Model II: Productive Reasoning*, or, more simply, *candid vulnerability*—in which individuals *candidly* share that hidden world of observations, inferences, and assumptions while also making that world *vulnerable* to examination, critique, and invalidation by others.

The first process—defensive reasoning—leads to interpersonal conflict and collective concealment. The second process—candid vulnerability—leads to interpersonal dialogue and collective transparency. Unfortunately, the developers at TIM Group realized that they were still experiencing domination and conflict because they were mired in defensive reasoning—and that if self-management was going to work for them, they would have to figure out a way to embrace candid vulnerability.

Defensive Reasoning versus Candid Vulnerability

How many times have you sat through a meeting where everyone smiles and nods their heads in agreement, yet afterward they gather in small groups to privately voice complaints, reservations, even outrage? How many times have you tentatively voiced a concern in a meeting only to see the recipient of that concern skillfully avoid addressing it while quickly steering the conversation onto a new topic? (And how many times have you done the exact same thing when someone voices a concern to you?)

These are all examples of a pattern of behavior known as *defensive reasoning*. It's a way of thinking, speaking, and acting designed to maintain control within a group while avoiding negative feelings, embarrassments, and threats. According to Chris Argyris, an internationally renowned sociologist and psychologist whose research changed our understanding of organizational behavior, defensive reasoning boils down to four basic routines:[1]

- **"Be in unilateral control."** When advocating for your position in a group, maintain control over the conversation so that it does not threaten your position or slip away onto a different path.
- **"Win and do not lose."** Although you may care about whether or not your position is right or true, you care more about ensuring that your position carries the day, regardless of whether it was truly the best path forward.
- **"Suppress conflict."** Many of us are taught as children, "If you don't have anything nice to say, then say nothing at all." As adults, we often end up censoring our thoughts, feelings, and concerns out of fear for how other people may choose to react to them.
- **"Behave rationally."** Whenever challenged, we have a deep and abiding desire to appear rational. We seek to justify our

positions and behaviors as logical and necessary, even if the reality is that our behaviors are irrational, contradictory, and self-defeating.

According to Argyris, we unconsciously employ these four routines whenever we engage in defensive reasoning. To illustrate, let's take another look at those hypothetical meeting scenarios at the start of this section.

If, while advocating for your position during a meeting, you skillfully avoid exploring or addressing the concerns of others, you are enacting defensive routine #1—*maintain unilateral control*—as well as defensive routine #2—*win and do not lose*. Similarly, when you smile and nod your head in agreement during a meeting yet afterward privately voice complaints, reservations, and even outrage to sympathetic ears, you are enacting defensive routine #3—*suppress conflict*. Lastly, whenever you tell yourself that these are the only rational things to do in these situations, you are enacting routine #4—*behave rationally*.

Defensive reasoning routines lead to the propagation and preservation of individual and organizational dysfunction. They are the reason the same conflicts break out quarter after quarter despite the persistent efforts of managers to deal with recurring organizational woes. They are the reason people complain privately to each other about recurring organizational and interpersonal problems yet publicly cooperate in sweeping these problems under the rug. In other words, defensive routines cause organizations to become stuck—and the people within them to feel trapped.

Sociologists have found that defensive reasoning is the overwhelming basis for group behavior all over the world. According to a global sociological study by Chris Argyris and others, we can find these routines in adults regardless of whether they are "young or old, female or male, minority or majority, wealthy or poor, well-educated or poorly educated."[2]

Yet, if you asked the typical adult whether or not their actions were animated by the four defensive routines listed above, chances are they would deny it—vehemently. In fact, sociologists have found that most individuals espouse a very different set of beliefs and preferred behaviors for interactions within groups in contradiction to the observed behaviors. These espoused behaviors (or routines) are as follows:[3]

- **"Seek valid, testable information."** Instead of maintaining control over a discussion in order to ensure your position carries the day, you should seek out information that may validate or invalidate the particular approach that you are advocating.

- **"Create informed choice within groups."** Groups are constantly faced with choices, in which different people within the group advocate for different paths to follow. In order to create *informed* choice, we should share the underlying observations, inferences, and assumptions that lead us to advocate for our ideas in the first place.
- **"Monitor vigilantly to detect and correct errors in our approach."** Just because a group chooses a path does not mean the path was the right one. We should look for flaws or errors in our approach and, if we find them, we should be willing to admit that we've made a mistake.

If followed, these three routines lead to candid vulnerability because they're all about collective learning instead of individual control. To illustrate, imagine you are a nontechnical product manager on a software team faced with a "pivot or persevere" moment. Your teammates seem somewhat evenly divided on what to do, and you find yourself advocating for the team to pivot the product onto a different path, focused on a different opportunity. Although you openly share a number of business justifications for pivoting with the team, you also harbor a number of hidden fears and motivations—like a fear that the engineers on the team are too inexperienced to tackle the product's current focus. You also personally find a different opportunity more interesting than the product's current focus.

Had you enacted the routines of defensive reasoning, you would have kept both your personal interests and your concerns about engineering prowess to yourself. But by following the routines of candid vulnerability, you share your hidden fears and personal motivations with others on the team so the team can make an informed choice about whether to pivot or persevere.

When you share the observations that caused you concern about the team's engineering prowess, you discover that you misinterpreted the situation due to your own nontechnical background. But you also discover that several other people on the team were growing increasingly disinterested in the product's current focus. In other words, by candidly sharing the hidden thoughts, feelings, and assumptions behind your preference to pivot—and by making them vulnerable to collective examination, critique, and invalidation—you created the conditions for the team to make an informed choice about how best to proceed.

The routines of candid vulnerability are a powerful antidote to the habits of defensive reasoning that we have all learned from birth. When followed, candid vulnerability leads people to share their inner thoughts, observations, assumptions, and theories about others to test their veracity. It also leads people to adjust their behaviors and beliefs when they discover errors in their thinking.

Although most people, in most organizations, espouse candid vulnerability, few demonstrate it in practice. Which is part of what makes radically collaborative organizations so special—they don't just value candid vulnerability; they live it.

As the *HOW Report* notes, members of radically collaborative organizations "communicate transparently, engage in dialogue, share the truth (even when it's difficult), and make job, organizational performance, and other information broadly and readily available."[4] They also "give honest feedback, challenge majority opinions, and call out misconduct or actions inconsistent with the organization's values."[5]

In other words, radically collaborative organizations have somehow managed to create not just a few select individuals capable of skillfully exhibiting candid vulnerability—they've created entire cultures in which candid vulnerability is the norm. Let's now return to TIM Group to see just how they've managed this impressive, and all too rare, feat.

Candid Vulnerability in Practice

The Eight Behaviors

When the developers at TIM Group began to look for the mindsets and behaviors they would need to complete their transformation toward radical collaboration, they found the paper *Eight Behaviors for Smarter Teams*, by Roger Schwarz. Schwarz is a noted organizational psychologist and consultant, a former student of Chris Argyris, and the author of several influential books about effective teams.

In his *Eight Behaviors* paper, Schwarz distills several of the principles and practices that his books cover in more depth. Two specific elements in that paper had a dramatic impact on the culture of TIM Group: the eight behaviors themselves, as well as a technique for practicing candid vulnerability. Let's look at each of these in turn.

First, as the title of the paper indicates, Schwarz lists out eight behaviors that effective teams embrace:[6]

1. State views and ask genuine questions.
2. Share all relevant information.
3. Use clear examples and agree on what important words mean.
4. Explain reasoning and intent.
5. Focus on interests, not positions.
6. Test assumptions and inferences.
7. Jointly design next steps.
8. Discuss undiscussable issues.

These eight behaviors are Schwarz's attempt to elaborate on the three espoused behaviors (routines) of candid vulnerability—and they gave the developers at TIM Group a pragmatic way to overcome dominator habits within teams. After laminating these behaviors onto cards and posting them around the workplace, the developers began to turn to them whenever dominator habits became apparent.

As one TIM Group employee told me, "Quite often during meetings, when people could sense that the interactions weren't going well, they'd pick up the card and start working through it, asking themselves, 'What behavior do I need?'"

For example, if someone felt like their team was dodging or avoiding a potentially divisive issue, they would remind themselves to follow behavior #8: "discuss undiscussable issues," in other words, to speak *candidly*.

Similarly, if they found themselves avoiding questions or criticisms of their position, they would remind themselves to "share all relevant information" and to "explain reasoning and intent"—thereby making their positions *vulnerable*.

Finally, whenever anyone seemed to be taking unilateral control over the team's direction, they would all remind themselves to "jointly design next steps."

Of course, it's one thing to know that you need to exhibit a certain behavior. It's quite another to understand *how* to exhibit it. As Chris Argyris repeatedly cautions in his books, it's not enough to endorse candid vulnerability—we have to practice it, like any other skill. That's why the developers at TIM Group picked up something else from the *Eight Behaviors* paper, the *two-column exercise*.

The Two-Column Exercise

The idea behind the two-column exercise is simple. Draw a line down the middle of a blank piece of paper, dividing it into two columns. In the right-hand column, write down the words of a conversation that recently occurred between you and someone else. In the left-hand column, write down what you were thinking during the conversation. The discrepancies between what you privately thought and publicly shared can be illuminating.

For most of us, the difference between the two columns reveals a tremendous amount of defensive reasoning. For example, we might discover that we suppress our honest thoughts, feelings, and beliefs from others to avoid negative emotions, protect self-images, and maintain unilateral control. We likewise might discover that our hidden thoughts reveal a story that we tell ourselves about others—about their intentions and motivations. We also might find that we never openly share our story with others and thus never verify its integrity. For all we might know, the story is nothing more than an elaborate fiction—yet hiding that story is part and parcel of defensive reasoning.

The two-column exercise is a way to reveal to everyone to what extent your thinking is enmeshed in defensive reasoning—which is the first and necessary step to overcoming it. But you can take the exercise further. Once you examine the delta between your private thoughts and your public proclamations, you can begin to practice candid vulnerability by rewriting the conversation.

Instead of hiding your real thoughts and feelings, you can safely imagine ways to candidly share those thoughts while making them vulnerable to critique. In other words, you can practice ways to tell others the story that you tell yourself.

This is exactly what the developers at TIM Group did. Whenever they felt like an interaction went wrong, they would use the two-column exercise to help them determine how they could have exhibited candid vulnerability instead of defensive reasoning. Although they couldn't rewrite the past through this exercise, they could prepare for the future. By working out alternative responses and inquiries, they were more likely to draw on those alternatives the next time they found themselves in a similar interpersonal situation.

Jeffrey Fredrick, the CTO of TIM Group, found the practice so successful that he went on to coauthor a book about how to incorporate it into an agile transformation: *Agile Conversations: Transform Your Conversations, Transform Your Culture*.

Using the Advice Process to Practice Candid Vulnerability

Two-column exercises aren't the only way to practice candid vulnerability. The advice process that we've seen at Haufe-umantis is another way to work those muscles.

As a reminder, the advice process gives anyone in an organization the power to make a decision but it also increases the psychological energy needed to do so. That's because instead of making decisions unilaterally, people must seek out the thoughts, advice, questions, and criticisms of those who would be affected by the decision.

Although there's no requirement for the decision-maker to take anyone else's advice, the intent is nonetheless clear: invite vulnerability in the decision makers by exposing the chain of inferences that are leading them to make the decision in the first place.

Axel Singler, at Haufe-umantis, points to this chain of interactions as one of the primary values of the advice process for an organization transitioning from hierarchy to heterarchy. It helps leaders transition from defensive reasoning to candid vulnerability by developing their muscle memory for collaborative decision-making.

Biggest Fail of the Week

cLabs offers up another practice for increasing candid vulnerability within an organization: a meeting prompt they call the "biggest fail of the week." Typically used at the outset of a meeting, it gives everyone the chance to take turns sharing a failure they were personally involved in. Failures could range from the innocuous, like forgetting about a meeting, to the unfortunate, like discovering that your latest Lean experiment failed, to the sensitive, like realizing that a conflict boiled over because you had tried to suppress it instead of addressing it.

The point of the exercise isn't to beat yourself up over your mistakes but rather to celebrate your willingness to admit to them, learn from them, and share them with others. This culture of celebration is important—because when we celebrate these moments, we increase the energy available for candid vulnerability within the organization, thanks to a phenomenon known as *psychological success*.

Psychological Success

The concept of psychological success was first articulated in the 1940s by a group of psychologists studying a phenomenon known as "aspiration diversity." In a nutshell, aspiration diversity says that when we are presented with hard or even impossible tasks, many of us will formulate intermediate goals as a stepping stone—what researchers refer to as an individual's "momentary level of aspiration."

Yet that momentary aspiration level can vary widely from human to human. In attempting to account for this diversity, the researchers found a strong correlation between a momentary level of aspiration and the degree of psychological success and failure a subject had previously experienced.[7] As Argyris explains, "the amount of psychological energy people have for any task is strongly influenced by the degree of psychological success and failure they experience. The more psychological success, the more energy available."[8]

This not only helps explain why candid vulnerability is rare but why practices like the "biggest fail" are effective. It takes a lot of psychological energy to share your thoughts, feelings, beliefs, and assumptions and make them vulnerable to examination, critique, and even invalidation. We need ways to offset that energy investment—and celebrating the "biggest fail of the week" is a fantastic way to do just that. It turns a situation that would normally threaten our self-image and drain us of our psychological energy into an experience of deficiency gratification that replenishes our psychological energy and honors us for the fallible human being that we are.

When you create a culture in which sharing failure *increases* psychological success, you create an energy reservoir for further acts of candid vulnerability. That being said, outright celebration of candid vulnerability isn't the only way to increase psychological success. Practices that merely create space for openness and vulnerability have a similar effect because being seen and acknowledged is, on its own, a deficiency-gratifying experience.

Practices to Increase Psychological Success

Several practices from the last chapter fit this bill. For example, when colleagues at CivicActions begin meetings by sharing their balance scores with each other, they are normalizing openness and vulnerability. Even though colleagues at CivicActions do not name the factors behind their balance scores, they still exhibit courage when they honestly and openly share them—particularly when those scores are low.

For most of us, when we go to work, we hide our underlying emotional states from each other. We smile and pretend as if everything is okay, even if that's far from the truth. But balance scores break that habit by giving everyone a way to safely bring more of their true self into their interactions with others—and to have that vulnerability acknowledged, protected, and honored.

Check-ins are yet another practice that invites candid vulnerability while simultaneously *increasing* psychological success. When employees in Holacracy-powered organizations like cLabs begin governance meetings by sharing, or "checking in," their individual distractions, they create a "sacred space" for people to bring their full selves into the moment. Although check-ins require more psychological energy than simply providing a balance score, they also invite more empathy and understanding from peers. When colleagues safely share their troubles, they increase the ability for their peers to empathize with their challenges and adjust to their mental states—which, in turn, increases everyone's psychological success.

Spontaneous Candid Vulnerability

Each of the preceding practices are structured activities designed to practice and/or elicit candid vulnerability at planned moments. But *structured* practices are only a stepping stone—a "momentary level of aspiration," if you will. The real ideal is pervasive, *spontaneous* candid vulnerability. When people spontaneously yet skillfully share their "undiscussable" thoughts, inferences, and assumptions, and open them up to testing and invalidation, structured practices for candid vulnerability become less necessary. Let's look at how this spontaneity has manifested in some of the organizations we have studied so far.

In previous chapters, we saw how Matt Black Systems developed one of the most devolved organizations on the planet. The employees of Matt Black Systems increasingly took over ownership and control of the organization, based on a fractal model of organizational design in which every employee became a virtual company of one. But they also increasingly developed a culture of candid vulnerability that made their new values of individual entrepreneurship and transparency possible. This culture of openness not only animated everyday interactions, it also enabled the organization to spontaneously self-organize in response to unexpected setbacks.

For instance, several years after their self-managing culture took effect, a fire beset the factory. The owners, who had not stepped foot in the factory for some time, showed up to survey the damage with the workers. One of the owners, sensing the need to take control, began to bark orders at everyone. But instead of reverting into a command-and-control hierarchy, the employees candidly told him that his actions weren't necessary; that they knew better than anyone how to cope with the situation since they knew better than anyone how to get the factory back up and running.[9]

Through the fractal organizational model, the employees themselves had been responsible for not only designing and producing products but for managing lease agreements, negotiating insurance contracts, securing loans, and purchasing equipment. As a result, they knew how to manage through this crisis—and they were better poised to do so. In a moment of vulnerability, the owner admitted to his mistake, apologized, and stepped aside. He then watched as the workers got the factory up to a minimally productive state in just three days by self-organizing in response to the catastrophe and employing innovative usages of the surviving machinery.[10]

The crisis demonstrates the power of candid vulnerability. Instead of regressing back into a dominator hierarchy, Matt Black Systems grew to new heights of partnership and equality. But the crisis also illustrates the leadership philosophy at work within radically collaborative organizations: leadership is contextual. It is governed by the situation, not the org chart. And it is granted by the trust of peers, not by the fiat of a dominator hierarchy. When a leader emerges within a heterarchy, they embody the ancient democratic ideal of *primus inter pares*, or "first among equals." And when the moment has passed and their leadership is no longer needed, practices like candid vulnerability ensure that their leadership ends with empathy and grace.

Matt Black Systems isn't the only pioneer to demonstrate candid vulnerability in a challenging situation. Thanks to tenets like the eight behaviors and practices like the two-column exercise, TIM Group also developed the ability to leverage candor and vulnerability at critical moments. For example, in 2018, the founders of TIM Group organized a surprise all-hands meeting in which they announced that the company was being acquired. Although there was a significant financial upside for the founders, the employees were facing the prospect of substantial change, instability, and assimilation into a parent company that may or may not have any interest in the radically collaborative culture that the employees had worked so hard to cultivate.

In most organizations, this disconnect would be "undiscussable," and the town hall would be dominated by owners eager to paint a rosy picture for everyone. At TIM Group, however, this undiscussable topic came out into the open. When one employee began by stating, "It sounds like selling the company isn't a win for everyone," the mood in the room quickly shifted into one of openness and sharing. People became able to openly name their fears and apprehensions and the underlying narratives that animated them. Even the founders were able to skillfully participate, as they had, over the years, embraced the tenets of candid vulnerability and had even participated in, and later led, trainings on how to run activities like the two-column exercise.

To sum up, the members of TIM Group had learned how to "discuss the undiscussable." They could bring up topics that they held back out of fear for the negative feelings they might generate in others or for the critiques they might inflict upon themselves. And they could productively engage in those conversations by candidly sharing the chain of inferences, thoughts, assumptions, and beliefs behind the undiscussable topic, thus opening that chain to testing, invalidation, and collective evolution.

Discussing the undiscussable doesn't guarantee a resolution to every dilemma, of course, but the experience of productively and skillfully examining undiscussables in a company-wide town hall illustrates the powerful potential that candid vulnerability holds—not just for individuals but for organizations as a whole.

In the case of TIM Group, candid vulnerability didn't stop the acquisition but it did allow the organization to have a better, smoother, and more engaged transition to new ownership, and gave everyone the ability to make an informed choice about whether or not they would like to join the acquiring company or leave.

CivicActions provides another example of spontaneous candor and vulnerability. During the spring and summer of 2020, the US was reeling from the COVID-19 pandemic and from the recent murders of unarmed Black people at the hands of police. The murders of George Floyd and Breonna Taylor, specifically, set off a wave of protests at state capitols around the nation. People of color were hurting, and the mood inside CivicActions reflected this.

During one especially momentous week full of protests around the US, the CivicAction's leadership team decided that the weekly all-hands meeting should create a space for people to share their pain, suffering, and anger openly. Aaron Pava also thought it was important for leadership to protect this space by refraining from participation and instead only listening. At the time, it sounded like a good plan; in retrospect, it was a mistake.

Although the call did allow people to share their pain and anger, Pava learned afterward that the Black community at CivicActions had interpreted the silence from leadership as a lack of support. He felt terrible. This was the exact opposite of what Pava had intended. He wanted to make sure that everyone at CivicActions knew that leadership supported the Black Lives Matter movement, so he and the other executives crafted a public statement to that effect. He pushed it out through social media and then reposted it internally—only to realize that he had made matters worse.

The internal critique was immediate. The statement was seen as hollow and virtue-signaling. Although it condemned white supremacy, it did little more. It didn't signal-boost Black voices, internal or external. It didn't provide any specific support or guidance for people wanting to take action. And in crafting it, Pava had not involved the Diversity, Equity, and Inclusion Peer Group at CivicActions.

He now felt devastated. With the best of intentions, Pava had made a bad situation worse. So, in a moment of vulnerability, he wrote a letter to the company. In it, Pava admitted to his mistakes, genuinely thanked everyone for their willingness to call him out on it, and also reflected back to everyone the suggestions that he had heard. Colleagues at CivicActions again responded immediately—but this time with love, support, and thanks. Now they felt heard. Now they felt supported. Now they felt like they could collectively develop a genuine response to the growing crisis of racism in America.

Their willingness to speak uncomfortable truths, combined with Pava's willingness to be vulnerable and open about his failure, allowed the organization to come together and genuinely craft a path forward. That's the promise of candid vulnerability. It's not about creating a perfect organization. It's about embracing the imperfections that humanity entails.

Conclusion

As we've seen throughout this chapter, there are two predominant modes of reasoning individuals engage in within groups: defensive reasoning and candid vulnerability. Defensive reasoning is composed of a set of routines designed to help individuals maintain unilateral control over a group while avoiding situations that might expose flaws or defects within their stated positions. On the other hand, candid vulnerability is composed of a set of psychological routines that help an individual expose gaps, shortcomings, and outright inaccuracies in their chain of inferences in the service of collective learning, creativity, and success.

Most individuals and organizations are enmeshed in a quagmire of defensive reasoning often precipitated by (and indicative of) the dynamics of domination and coercion. The same conflicts break out quarter after quarter, despite management's best efforts to resolve them. Organizational dysfunctions are privately complained about yet publicly swept under the rug.

Radically collaborative organizations, in contrast, exhibit candid vulnerability in their daily routines—and their experiences, surveyed in this chapter, illustrate its power. By giving individuals the courage to expose their beliefs to collective examination, candid vulnerability liberates teams to choose new directions based on valid information instead of being held captive by individual egos.

Similarly, giving individuals the strength to discuss the undiscussable, candid vulnerability gives organizations the power to overcome the dysfunctions that traditional organizations find themselves interminably saddled with. And finally, by creating structured ways to practice candid vulnerability on a daily basis, radically collaborative organizations have, over time, been able to manifest it spontaneously, with increasing frequency, complexity, and impact.

Although spontaneous candid vulnerability is the goal, its attainment isn't guaranteed to last. That's because organizations aren't static. They grow, shrink, and change over time. New members join; old members leave. And what is gained can also be lost. There will always be a place and a need for structured practices like two-column exercises and Holacractic check-ins, because it is those practices that maintain a culture of openness amid all the flux, and that sustain the downstream multiplier effects on organizational agility. They are also what renews the potential that candid vulnerability holds for individual fulfillment and well-being. When we create a culture of candid vulnerability, we don't just help our organizations survive in an uncertain world—we help each other thrive as the uncertain, fallible, beautiful human beings we are.

Questions for Reflection:

» Can you think of a moment in which someone within your organization has engaged in defensive reasoning? In which they have hidden their underlying thoughts and feelings in an attempt to maintain control, to win, to suppress conflict, or to appear rational?

» Now that you have identified defensive reasoning in someone else, can you do the same for yourself? In other words, can you think of a moment in your life in which you have hidden your underlying thoughts and feelings in an attempt to maintain control, to win, to suppress conflict, or to appear rational?

» Now that you have an example of defensive reasoning in yourself, can you imagine what you might have done differently in order to display candid vulnerability? How you could have made your underlying thoughts, feelings, assumptions, and beliefs open to examination, critique, and even invalidation?

» Where do you believe your organization falls on the spectrum between defensive reasoning and candid vulnerability? And, more importantly, what are the chain of observations, inferences, and assumptions that lead you to this belief? Are you willing to candidly share that chain of thought with others, thereby making it vulnerable?

» What could you do to increase the likelihood that people will choose candor and vulnerability on teams and in meetings instead of suppression and control? In other words, how can you make candid vulnerability more attractive to yourself and others while simultaneously making defensive reasoning less attractive?

A RADICAL ENTERPRISE

Most readers will be familiar with the film *The Truman Show* about the life of Truman Burbank, a man who has grown up within a vast simulated reality. Quite unbeknownst to him, everyone who surrounds him, including his wife, is an actor, and hidden cameras broadcast his every moment to the rest of the world. He has never left the island community in which he was raised, and although the creators of his simulated world have attempted to provide him with a good life, he is nonetheless beset with feelings of unease and disaffection. In time, he decides to leave his hometown, and after a failed escape attempt, he manages to evade the authorities and sail out onto open water. To his surprise, his small boat runs into a wall that looks just like a cloud, and he discovers a staircase that leads up to a door that can take him out of his simulated reality and into the real world.

He pauses on the stairway and faces a choice. Should he go back to the simulated reality, the only reality he's ever known, with its allure of apparent safety and dependable routine, or should he open the door and venture out into a new world?

This poignant moment deeply resonated with audiences, and, odd though it may sound, I believe it is not without parallel to the situation that we knowledge workers find ourselves in now as the global pandemic, hopefully, draws to a close.

Most of us have grown up in industrialized nations and have enjoyed lives of relative stability. We've been raised to believe that our communities, organizations, and governments are the best in the world, and that the underlying socioeconomic structures and paradigms are to thank for their superiority.

Yet something is wrong. In spite of all that we have been told, we are plagued by feelings of disaffection. We experience a daily reality of disengagement, mistrust, meaninglessness, and insecurity thanks to the paradigm of domination and coercion that we have spent our lives operating within.

But now, because of the COVID-19 pandemic, we've glimpsed another way of working. We've experienced a greater sense of autonomy and equality in our work, and we've gained a new level of control over our lives and lived experiences. And so we, like Truman, face a choice. Do we go back to the way things were—to the dominator hierarchies that have constituted our daily reality for nearly all of our lives? Or do we move forward into a new world, one grounded in partnership and equality and centered around a radical collaboration that flows from the intrinsic motivation of peers and the free commitments of participants?

Truman had to make his choice with no knowledge of what stood on the other side of the door. We are, however, more fortunate. Radically collaborative organizations already exist for us to either join or model ourselves after, and this book has surveyed their practices and distilled their essence down into four essential elements: team autonomy, managerial devolution, deficiency gratification, and candid vulnerability.

> **Team autonomy.** Radically collaborative organizations feature a radical approach to collaboration based on intrinsic motivation and freedom of commitment. Radical collaborators join teams filled with people *who* they want to collaborate with. They collectively work out *how* to work together and *what* to work on. They decide *where* to work and whether they're collocated or distributed, just as they decide *when* to work, synchronously or asynchronously. And lastly, they choose what *role* to play, by considering both organizational needs and individual goals and aspirations. By establishing these six dimensions of autonomy—the *how*, *what*, *who*, *when*, *where*, and *role*—radically collaborative organizations create the conditions for everyone to find meaning and fulfillment in their work. And by aligning intrinsic motivation with organizational need, radically collaborative organizations create workforces with superior levels of engagement and productivity.

> **Managerial devolution.** Radically collaborative organizations are formed and maintained through managerial devolution—i.e., through the decentralization of power out of a static dominator hierarchy and into a dynamic heterarchy of self-managing teams. These teams are founded on the concepts of partnership and equal-

ity, and they are united in the belief that leadership is dynamic and contextual—i.e., that it is granted by the trust of peers and limited to the situation at hand. Radical collaborators collectively evolve the organizational structure through devolutionary management practices like the advice process, ad hoc leadership teams, and Holacracy-powered governance. They self-manage hiring, onboarding, firing, etc. And they even self-manage compensation through devolutionary systems like the fractal organizational model, the Deming Pay System, and self-managed pay. Managerial devolution is a boon for organizational agility. By devolving management out of a dominator hierarchy and into the organization at large, radically collaborative organizations can sense and respond to tensions and adapt to new socioeconomic conditions with a rapidity that their hierarchical competitors can only dream of.

Deficiency gratification. The most monumental discovery of the twentieth century wasn't the theory of relativity or the discovery of DNA. It was the discovery that humans have needs that other animals don't. Like all animals, we need sun, water, food, and air. But unlike other animals, we also need security, autonomy, fairness, esteem, trust, and belongingness. Provided these needs, we thrive; deprived of them, we wither. Dominator hierarchies lead to economically disastrous levels of worker disaffection because they systematically threaten our basic human needs. They are, *by design*, deficiency-inducing, growth-inhibiting structures. But radically collaborative organizations create the conditions for the repeated gratification of human needs. Through a mix of social structures and daily practices, radical collaborators give each other autonomy, fairness, and esteem, and cocreate environments of security, trust, and belongingness. This isn't just a boon for individual well-being and fulfillment—it's a proven multiplier for organizational performance. By creating high levels of interpersonal trust, radically collaborative environments exhibit thirty-two times the risk-taking, eleven times the innovation, and six times the business performance over their hierarchical peers.[1] Thanks to results like these, we now know that we don't have to choose between the well-being of individuals and the success of corporations. The former is, in fact, a multiplier of the latter.

Candid vulnerability. While dominator hierarchies are ensnared in a quagmire of defensive reasoning—in which people hide and defend their underlying assumptions and beliefs from others in an attempt to maintain unilateral control—radically collaborative organizations sparkle with openness and transparency thanks to their cultures of *candid vulnerability*. In these organizations, radical collaborators candidly share and skillfully discuss their underlying thoughts, feelings, beliefs, and assumptions, thereby making their thought processes vulnerable to collective examination, critique, and invalidation. This in turn creates the grounds for individual growth and collective innovation. By untethering ideas from their ego-sources, candid vulnerability enables individuals to grow through the rapid discovery of self-knowledge, and it enables organizations to innovate through the rapid exploration and testing of ideas.

The four imperatives of radical collaboration blend into an overall archetype that gives me hope for the nature of work and the future of humanity. In contrast to organizations that claim to be progressive, touting humanistic benefits and generous salaries while doing nothing to address the underlying system of domination and coercion that their organization is built upon, the four imperatives make plain that real radical collaboration begins where paternalistic benefits end.

Radically collaborative workplaces are characterized not by perk and privilege but by the meaningful experience of partnership and equality, formed through the devolution of management and sustained through intrinsic motivation and freedom of commitment. (That's not to say radically collaborative organizations are bereft of benefits but rather that benefits that exist within them are due to the devolutionary choices of the radical collaborators themselves, as opposed to the beneficence of dominators.)

On a similar note: among traditional corporations, sustainable business practices are the exception rather than the norm, but it's easy to imagine that the opposite would be true for radically collaborative organizations. Since an organization's external relationships are an extension of their internal structures, radical collaboration and sustainability should go hand in hand—and there's even some compelling data to back that up.

According to the *HOW Report*, over 90% of radically collaborative organizations exhibit sustainable business practices (compared to 33% of hierarchical corporations), just as 96% of radically collaborative corporations exhibit a commitment to social and environmental issues (compared to 32% of hierarchical corporations).[2] These results suggest that just as radical collaborators build their internal relationships on a vision of partnership and equality, so too do they naturally view their external relationships through that same lens.

Thus, the imperatives taken together with the empirical results presented throughout this book make a compelling argument that dominator hierarchies are neither necessary nor even advantageous—which leads me to end this book with two questions.

First: What will it take to create a whole world full of radically collaborative, deficiency-gratifying organizations? And second: What will happen to the human being after a prolonged immersion within a radically collaborative environment?

A World of Radical Collaboration

We'll begin with the first question. As we have previously noted, 8% of the world's corporations are already well within the radically collaborative spectrum—a number that has grown and is continuing to grow rapidly.[3]

Still, it's a long way from 8% to 100%. So, what will it really take to get there? What needs to happen to truly end the tyranny of domination and coercion and replace it with a foundation of deficiency gratification and candid vulnerability in which work becomes not an encumbrance of stress and strife but a self-renewing wellspring of joy, meaning, and fulfillment? Given the economic superiority of radically collaborative organizations, is it just a matter of time before they transform every industry and nation around the world? Or is something else needed beyond pure economics?

I have to admit that I don't know the answer. But I have an educated guess.

How did dominator hierarchies become the predominant organizational paradigm on the planet? How did domination and coercion become the intuitive, go-to techniques for organizing human production and sociality? Did someone go around with a petition asking people to sign their names in support of the tyranny of domination? Did people organize marches, vigils, and sit-ins to convince others of the need for dominator hierarchies? Or did Congress pass a bill to require them or create laws to maintain and enforce them?

Clearly, the answer is no. Dominator hierarchies naturally form and naturally sustain themselves without explicit catalysts to create them or explicit programs to enforce or maintain them. That's because they are the natural outcropping of a dominator *mindset*. And that mindset is programmed into us from birth—not by biological genes but by cultural *memes*.

No, I'm not referring to those funny images and captions that pepper the internet—at least not principally. I'm referring to the theory of cultural propagation that Richard Dawkins first introduced and articulated in his book *The Selfish Gene*.[4] Memes are self-replicating units of culture that silently yet powerfully shape our world. They are the ideas, beliefs, assumptions, and dispositions that underlie our behaviors and they transmit from person to person through language, symbols, and actions. When we speak with each other, work with each other, play with each other, and fight with each other, we transmit memes between us. Parents pass memes onto children—but so do teachers and coaches, friends and enemies, books and television. We are silently, invisibly, and *unrelentingly* bathed in memes from birth, and our entire being is coated with them.

Memes are the reason that dominator hierarchies flourish in our world. They're the reason that people intuitively reach for domination and coercion when organizing human activity. We've been taught from birth that people must be cajoled with privileges and punishments, grades and gold stars, bonuses and performance evaluations—for without carrots and sticks human activity would grind to a halt and our modern world would fall apart. These are the memes we have learned from our earliest moments in this world—and these are the lies that our world is built upon every day.

One of my favorite authors, Daniel Quinn, likened memes to a river. He said that the memes of our culture—the memes of domination and coercion, patriarchy and misogyny, racism and white supremacy, material consumption and environmental degradation—weave together into a vast, flowing river, winding inexorably toward the end of the world. And he said that all of our programmatic efforts to stop it—all of our campaigns for ending poverty, crime, racism, sexism, famine, and environmental devastation—are as hopeless as sticks planted in the bed of a river to impede its flow.[5]

In other words, the world won't be saved by programs. What we need is a new river. One not polluted with memes like domination and coercion but rather purified with memes like deficiency gratification and candid vulnerability. One in which the natural flow is not toward misery and devastation but toward security, autonomy, fairness, esteem, trust, belongingness, and love. One in which people are not punished but honored and celebrated for bringing their full, authentic, imperfect, and beautiful human selves into each and every interaction with each other. What we need is a river of radical collaboration.

All rivers have a source. If you trace a river, no matter how big, you will eventually arrive at a small trickle of water seeping out of a crack and humbly yet persistently spilling onto the earth.

You are that source. You are the wellspring of deficiency gratification and candid vulnerability. You are the trickle of humanity that has the power to change the world. So spill away. Spill security, autonomy, fairness, esteem, trust, belongingness, and love out into the world. Spread your thoughts, feelings, beliefs, and assumptions to others and make them vulnerable to examination, critique, and invalidation. Be candid. Be caring. *Be radical!* And one day, with persistence and humility, radical collaboration will form a river so mighty that it will wash away all of the bullshit, heartache, and misery that domination and coercion have wrought upon the world—and no program of action will have the power to stop it.

Which now leads me to my second question. What will happen to the human being over time as they experience a prolonged immersion within that river—i.e., within a psychologically healthy environment in which their deficiency needs are repeatedly gratified and in which they become increasingly capable of making their inner thoughts, feelings, assumptions, and beliefs open to examination, critique, and invalidation?

The answer, as it turns out, is significant. According to the field of positive psychology, a human being immersed in a deficiency-gratifying environment for an extended period of time is likely to change in a fundamental way. As Maslow explains,

> Healthy people have sufficiently gratified their basic needs for safety, belongingness, love, respect, and self-esteem so that they are motivated primarily by trends to self-actualization (defined as ongoing actualization of potentials, capacities and talents, as fulfillment of mission [or call, fate, destiny, or vocation], as a fuller knowledge of,

and acceptance of, the person's own intrinsic nature, as an unceasing trend toward unity, integration or synergy within the person).[6]

Maslow goes on to elaborate that as deficiency needs subside, new needs with new forms and qualities emerge and press for gratification, including the need for simplicity, richness, essentiality, oughtness, beauty, wholeness, perfection, completion, uniqueness, dichotomy-transcendence, acceptance, resolution, integration, and even ending, finality, totality, cessation.[7]

Unlike deficiency needs, which must be gratified by interpersonal relationships, these new needs are largely gratified by the individual themself. "The self-actualizing individual, by definition gratified in his basic needs, is far less dependent, far less beholden, far more autonomous and self-directed . . . . The determinants which govern him are now primarily inner ones, rather than social or environmental . . . . In the later stages of growth, the person is essentially alone and can rely only upon himself."[8]

As gratification turns inward, a new attitude toward reality emerges, pervaded by feelings of "awe, love, adoration, worship, humility, feeling of smallness plus godlikeness, reverence, approval of, agreement with, wonder, sense of mystery, gratitude, devotion, dedication, identification with, belonging to, fusion with, surprise and incredulousness, fear, joy, rapture, bliss, ecstasy, etc."[9]

All of this culminates in a new state of cognition, known as "being-cognition," a "cognition of the essence, or 'is-ness,' or intrinsic structure and dynamics, and presently existing potentialities of something or someone or everything,"[10] which, in turn, correlates with a number of clinically observed characteristics in the individual, including "increased spontaneity," "increased acceptance of self, of others and of nature," "increased detachment and desire for privacy," as well as a "higher frequency of peak experiences."[11] In these peak experiences, "the world is totally forgotten," but "the ego is also totally forgotten."[12] We experience an unselfconscious sense of concreteness and clarity, unclouded by ego, and untethered from abstractions, in which perception becomes "all figure, and the ground, in effect, disappears."[13] These experiences are moments of actualization that simultaneously realize individual potential and yet transcend it, and they occur with increased frequency and impact in self-actualizing individuals.

Clearly, people like this are a rarity in our present societies. It is far more normal to experience psychopathology and deficiency motivation than it is to experience psychological health and being-motivation. So what will happen when we manage to create a whole world of radically collaborative organizations? When people all over the world begin to experience the prolonged and systemic basic need gratification that enables self-actualization, new states of being-motivation, and transcendence of environments? When individuals begin to, en masse, exhibit a "superior perception of reality," a "resistance to enculturation," and an "increased detachment and desire for privacy," as well as a "more democratic character structure," "increased spontaneity," and an "increased acceptance of self, of others, and of nature?"[14]

I feel no shame in admitting that I have absolutely no idea what would happen in this scenario. This state of being is so unlike anything we can point to in our everyday lives that predicting what a single individual might do in this state, much less a society of such individuals, seems like pure guesswork. Perhaps they would carry on creating and maintaining radically collaborative organizations. Perhaps they would discover whole new heights of being and sociality that make being-cognition and radical collaboration seem primitive and base in comparison. Who knows? Not me, certainly. But I can say this. Though I know not what will happen once we arrive at those farther reaches of human nature, I am absolutely committed to the destination and more than ready to start the journey. This book has been my first step. And if you are still with me, dear reader, I hope that it has been your first step too.

ACKNOWLEDGMENTS

When I wrote the final paragraphs of the last chapter, I cried. At the time, I didn't know why I was crying. Perhaps it was simply the catharsis of finishing. Although I wrote the manuscript for this book in eight weeks, I had been reading, researching, and writing for years. I have thousands of pages of notes, interviews, chapter fragments, and false starts. To have all of that finally coalesce into a coherent body of writing was both an achievement and a relief.

It's also possible that my tears were tears of exhaustion. I began this particular manuscript in January 2021, during the height of the COVID-19 pandemic. Although I had no job during that winter, my wife worked from home full time and our three children, aged two to ten, were with us twenty-four hours a day, seven days a week. I spent the daylight hours caring for our toddler, while also trying to keep our two older children signed on and engaged in their virtual classrooms.

Since it wasn't possible to work on my manuscript so long as our children were awake, I got up everyday at 4:00 AM and wrote through the wee hours while drinking dangerously large amounts of coffee. I'm naturally a morning person, so this proved possible. However, it didn't prove sustainable. By the time I finished the manuscript eight weeks later, I was sleep deprived beyond the help of caffeine. I *needed* to finish. In that light, perhaps tears were to be expected.

My tears may also have had something to do with isolation. A number of authors have described the writing process as lonely. Stephen King, for example, had this to say in his memoir: "Writing is a lonely job. Having someone who believes in you makes a lot of difference. They don't have to make speeches. Just believing is usually enough."[1] I've been fortunate enough to have lots of people who believe in me. My publisher, my editor, my friends, my family, and of course and most importantly of all, my wife and partner Nicole. Having that kind of love and support didn't eliminate the loneliness, but it certainly made it bearable. So maybe my tears were tears of gratitude for the support I have received and for the end to the self-imposed isolation that constitutes the writing process.

Catharsis. Exhaustion. Isolation. Gratitude. All of that undoubtedly contributed to my emotional state at the time. But as I reflect now, I realize that my tears were an experience of something else as well. My writing process is usually slow and halting, in which I laboriously transform my words, sentences, and paragraphs from jumbled and confused to ordered and precise. (This may partly explain why it has taken me years to complete this project.)

But unlike the rest of the manuscript, those final paragraphs flowed out of me abruptly. There was no hesitation over word choice, no puzzling over presentation or order. The ideas, metaphors, and messages rolled out my mind and off my fingertips as if fully formed. I began crying before I finished, but the words kept coming, unabated. For a moment, it was as if the room had faded away and nothing else remained save the characters appearing on my screen. My field of perception was "all figure, no ground," as Maslow would put it. In other words, finishing the manuscript was a "peak experience," a self-actualizing moment of realization and transcendence that was deeply meaningful and transformative—and I have many people to thank for it.

I'll begin with Rob Mee, the founder of Pivotal Labs and the eventual CEO of Pivotal Software. For reasons that I'll never understand, he asked me several years into my tenure at Pivotal Labs if I'd be interested in writing a book about Pivotal's ways of working. He did this on what seemed to me to be the spur of the moment, yet his willingness to take a chance on me has nonetheless altered the course of my life in ways both profound and profoundly fruitful. Although the particular book that he envisioned never quite came to fruition, and although Pivotal itself was not destined to last, Rob set me on a journey that has taken me to distant shores of knowledge and new horizons of being. I am forever grateful to him.

I'd also like to thank several of my fellow "pivots" (as Pivotal employees were called), including Rebecca Jean, Luke Winikates, Ben Christel, Joseph Palermo, Tom Kennedy, and Sam Mirza. An early, though ultimately abandoned, version of this manuscript detailed a week within the lives of these six "pivots" as they worked on radically collaborative teams. Their willingness to give me access to their experiences, emotions, thoughts, and sentiments during the course of a week, followed by in-depth interviews about their backgrounds, gave me new insights into the nature of radical collaboration that continue to influence me today. Although my writing eventually went in new directions that could no longer incorporate their experiences, I am indebted to them all for the time, knowledge, and experience they shared with me.

I'd also like to extend special thanks to another "pivot," Elisabeth Hendrickson, author of *Explore It! Reduce Risk and Increase Confidence with Exploratory Testing*. In addition to being a cherished mentor to me during my time at Pivotal, Elisabeth also introduced me to her friend and author, Gene Kim, and by extension, to the IT Revolution publishing company. Although I had a basic concept for the book and the beginnings of the manuscript, I was a first-time author. Without the belief and support of Elisabeth, you, my dear reader, would not be reading these words today.

My editor, Anna Noak, deserves my endless gratitude. She encouraged me, stuck with me, and leveled with me for years until I finally had a manuscript worthy of publication. As an author, I was a complete novice when I began with her, and although I know that I still have much to learn about the craft of writing, I also know that this manuscript has been improved immensely by her insights, suggestions, critiques, and clarifications.

There is a special place in my heart for my early readers: John Ryan, Phil Goodwin, and Wiley Kestner. They were kind enough to read this manuscript *before* Anna Noak applied her editorial gifts to it; and their critiques, insights, and reactions helped me not only understand where the text was weak, but also prepared me for the rewarding yet challenging task of developmental editing that lay ahead. Furthermore, since they read each chapter as soon as I completed it and since they quickly gave me feedback and encouragement, they became a deficiency-gratifying support group for me during the writing process, one that I could not have dispensed with. Thank you, my friends.

Lastly, I would like to thank my wife, Nicole, who has encouraged me, supported me, and counseled me along this journey every step of the way. She has been my first reader, my biggest fan, and my closest confidant throughout this process. Writing a book is a tremendous, almost absurd, investiture of time and impacts everything else within your life, including your job and your family. I could never have completed this book without Nicole's support and love. She is truly the O. G. radical collaborator.

RADICALLY COLLABORATIVE PIONEERS:
AT A GLANCE

Buurtzorg: Number one home health-care provider in the Netherlands. Fifteen-thousand colleagues. Founded in 2006 in the Netherlands, now in twenty-five countries. Broken up into thousands of small self-managing teams of nurses who self-manage everything from nursing, to hiring, to customer acquisition, and facilities.

CivicActions: Open-source government consultancy. One hundred people. Founded in 2004. One of the first fully distributed technology companies. Notable for decentralized, grassroots-organizing culture.

cLabs: Cryptocurrency company focused on creating the conditions for prosperity in developing communities around the world. One hundred fifty people. Founded 2018. Based in Berlin, Buenos Aires, and San Francisco. Notable for holacracy.

GrantTree: Helps organizations acquire government R&D grants. Sixty-five people. Founded in 2010. Based in London. Notable for pioneering self-managed pay.

Haier: Number one appliance manufacturer in the world. Eighty-thousand people. Founded in 1920. Notable for radically collaborative structure of self-managing microenterprises.

Haufe-umantis: Collaboration and talent-management software company. Two hundred people. Founded in 2002. Based in Switzerland. Notable for transitioning from dominator hierarchy, to workplace democracy, to self-management/radical collaboration.

Matt Black Systems: Manufacturer of airplane instruments. Thirty people. Founded 1973. Notable for fractal organizational model.

Morning Star: Largest tomato processor in the world. Four thousand people. Founded in 1990. No managers, no set roles or responsibilities. One hundred percent self-managing structure redesigned annually through CLOUs (colleague letters of understanding).

Nearsoft: A "nearshore" software consultancy in Mexico. 450 employees. Founded in 2006; acquired by Encora in 2020. Known for its "No" rules: No bosses. No "employees." No titles. No secrets. Motto: Freedom in the workplace.

Pod Group: Enterprise network operator (ENO) for Internet of Things. Twenty-five people. Based in San Francisco. Founded 1999. Notable for self-managing culture and self-managed pay.

TIM Group: Fintech focused on trade advice and investment recommendations. London-based. Acquired in 2018. Fifty-person self-managing group at time of acquisition. Notable for gradual, employee-led transformation toward radical collaboration via a management reading group.

Viisi: Fintech focused on mortgage advice. Forty people. Based in the Netherlands. Notable for implementing the Deming pay system.

W. L. Gore: Innovation organization focused on industrial and chemical innovation. Founded in 1958. Based in Delaware. Over eleven thousand employees. Revenues in excess of $3 billion. One of the first radically collaborative companies in the world. Open allocation process for teams and new innovation projects.

BIBLIOGRAPHY

Achor, Shawn, Andrew Reece, Gabriella Rosen Kellerman, and Alexi Robichaux. "9 Out of 10 People Are Willing to Earn Less Money to Do More Meaningful Work." *Harvard Business Review* (November 2018). https://hbr .org/2018/11/9-out-of-10-people-are-willing-to-earn-less-money-to-do -more-meaningful-work.

Analytics, Zogby. "2018 Job Seeker Nation Study: Researching the Candidate-Recruiter Relationship." Jobvite (April 2018). https://www.jobvite.com/wp -content/uploads/2018/04/2018_Job_Seeker_Nation_Study.pdf.

Argyris, Chris. *Organizational Traps*. New York: Jossey-Bass, 2010.

Argyris, Chris. *Overcoming Organizational Defenses*. New York: Jossey-Bass, 1990.

Arnold, Hermann. "Why We Have Replaced Leadership Elections in a Basic-Democratic Process with an Actual 'We are Boss.'" LinkedIn (June 12, 2020). https://www.linkedin.com/pulse/why-we-have-replaced-leadership -elections-manner-actual-arnold.

Asch, S. E. "Effects of Group Pressure on the Modification and Distortion of Judgments," in H. Guetzkow (ed), *Groups, Leadership and Men: Research in Human Relations*. Carnegie Press, 1951: 177–190.

Birkinshaw, Julian, Jordan Cohen, and Pawel Stach. "Research: Knowledge Workers are More Productive from Home." *Harvard Business Review* (August 2020). https://hbr.org/2020/08/research-knowledge-workers-are -more-productive-from-home.

Bruner, J. S., and L. J. Postman. "On the Perception of Incongruity: A Paradigm." *Journal of Personality* 18 (1949): 206–223.

"Buurtzorg: Revolutionising Home Care in the Netherlands." Centre for Public Impact (November 15, 2018). https://www.centreforpublicimpact.org /case-study/buurtzorg-revolutionising-home-care-netherlands.

"Chinese Industry Haier and Higher." *The Economist* (October 11, 2013). https://www.economist.com/business/2013/10/11/haier-and-higher.

Colvine, Sophie, and François Branthôme. "Top 50 Tomato Processing Companies Worldwide in 2020." Tomato News (March 16, 2021). https://www .tomatonews.com/en/top50-tomato-processing-companies-worldwide-in -2020_2_1295.html.

Crumley, Carole. "Heterarchy and the Analysis of Complex Societies." *Archaeological Papers of the American Anthropological Association* 6: 1–5. http//

www.researchgate.net/publication/227664129_Heterarchy_and_the
_Analysis_of_Complex_Societies/citation/download.

Consultancy.uk. "UK Employees Losing Faith in Annual Performance Management Cycles." Consultancy.uk (June 29, 2018). https://www.consultancy
.uk/news/17726/uk-employees-losing-faith-in-annual-performance
-management-cycles.

Damani, Fatema. "Pods: A Step Towards Self-Management." TIM-Group Dev
Blog (March 2017). https://devblog.timgroup.com/2017/03/21/pods-a
-step-towards-self-management.

Dawkins, Richard. *The Selfish Gene*. Oxford, England: Oxford University Press,
1976.

de Morree, Pim. "This Company Democratically Elects its CEO Every Single Year."
Corporate Rebels (December 2017). https: //corporate-rebels.com
/haufe-umantis/.

Deci, Edward L. "Effects of Externally Mediated Rewards on Intrinsic Motivation." *Journal of Personality and Social Psychology* 18 (1971): 105–115.

Deci, Edward, R. Koestner, and R. Ryan. "A Meta-Analytic Review of Experiments
Examining the Effects of Extrinsic Rewards on Intrinsic Motivation." *Psychological Bulletin* 125, no. 6 (1999): 627–668.

Deming, W. Edwards. *The Essential Deming: Leadership Principles from the
Father of Quality*. Edited by Joyce Nilsson Orsini. New York: McGraw Hill,
2013.

Deming, W. Edwards. *The New Economics: For Industry, Government, Education*. Second Edition. Cambridge, Massachusetts: MIT Press, 1994.

Deutschman, Alan. "The Fabric of Creativity." Fast Company (December 2004).
https://www.fastcompany.com/51733/fabric-creativity.

Dickler, Jessica. "'Great Resignation' Gains Steam as Return-to-Work Plans Take
Effect." CNBC (June 29, 2021). https://www.cnbc.com/2021/06/29/more
-people-plan-to-quit-as-return-to-work-plans-go-into-effect-.html.

Duffy, Kate. "Nearly 40% of Workers would Consider Quitting if Their
Bosses Made Them Return to the Office Full Time, a New Survey
Shows." *Business Insider* (June 2021). https://www.businessinsider.com/
quit-job-flexible-remote-working-from-home-return-to-office-2021-6.

Eisler, Riane. *The Chalice and the Blade*. New York: Harper One, 1987.

Eisler, Riane, and Lucy Garrick. "Leading the Shift from a Dominator to a
Partnership Culture." *The Systems Thinker* 19, no. 6 (2021). https://thesys-
temsthinker.com/leading-the-shift-from-a-dominator-to-a-partnership
-culture.

Fishman, Charles. "Engines of Democracy." Fast Company (September 1999).
https://www.fastcompany.com/37815/engines-democracy.

Glass, Robert. *Software Runaways: Monumental Software Disasters*. Prentice
Hall, 1997.

"Global Major Appliances Brand Rankings." Euromonitor, 2020.

Guetzkow, H. (ed), *Groups, Leadership and Men: Research in Human Rela-tions*. Carnegie Press, 1951.

Hamel, Gary, and Michele Zanini. *Humanocracy: Creating Organizations as Amazing as the People In Them*. Boston, Massachusetts: Harvard Business Review Press, 2020.

Hannah, Felicity. "'My Boss Lets Me Set My Own Salary.'" BBC News (September 13, 2019). https://www.bbc.com/news/business-49677147.

Hartner, Jim. "Dismal Employee Engagement Is a Sign of Global Mismanage-ment." Gallup (2018). https://www.gallup.com/workplace/231668 /dismal-employee-engagement-sign-global-mismanagement.aspx.

Hayes, M., F. Chumney, C. Wright, and M. Buckingham. "The Global Study of Engagement." ADP Research Institute, 2018. https://www.adp.com /-/media/adp/ResourceHub/pdf/ADPRI/ADPRI0102_2018_Engagement _Study_Technical_Report_RELEASE%20READY.ashx.

Holm, Andrew. "Fractal Model." FractalWork.com. Accessed September 16, 2021. https://fractalwork.com/fractal-model/.

Holm, Andrew. "From Time to Value." powerpoint presentation, December 2020. https://fractalwork.com/wp-content/uploads/2020/12/from-time-to-value-1.pdf.

Hornung, Stefanie. "Why We Should Not Punish Intrinsic Motivation." Corp-orate Rebels (March 2020). https://corporate-rebels.com/why-we-should -not-punish-intrinsic-motivation/.

Howington, Jessica. "Survey Explores Varying Attitudes of Millennials and Older Workers about Key Workplace Issues." Flexjobs (August 2018). https://www. flexjobs.com/blog/post/survey-finds-varying-attitudes-millennials-older -workers-about-key-workplace-issues.

Huang, G., H. Zhao, X. Niu, S. Ashford, and C. Lee. "Reducing Job Insecurity and Increasing Performance Ratings: Does Impression Management Matter?" *Journal of Applied Psychology* 98, no. 5 (2013): 333–378.

Hunt, J. M. *Personality and the Behavior Disorders*, 1944.

Irwin, Neil. "Unemployment Is High. Why Are Businesses Struggling to Hire?" *New York Times* (April 16, 2021). https://www.nytimes.com/2021/04/16 /upshot/unemployment-pandemic-worker-shortages.html.

Khubchandani, J., and J. H. Price. "Association of Job Insecurity with Health Risk Factors and Poorer Health in American Workers." *Journal of Community Health* 42 (2016): 242–251.

King, Stephen. *On Writing: A Memoir of the Craft*. New York: Scribner, 2000.

Kirkpatrick, Doug. *The No-Limits Enterprise: Organizational Self- Manage-ment in the New World of Work*. Charleston, South Carolina: Forbes Books, 2019.

Kohn, Alfie. *Punished By Rewards: The Trouble with Gold Stars, Incentive Plans, A's, Praise, and Other Bribes*. Twenty-Fifth Anniversary Edition. New York: Mariner Books, 2018.

Laloux, Frederic. *Reinventing Organizations: A Guide to Creating Organizations Inspired By the Next Stage of Human Consciousness*. Brussels, Belgium: Nelson Parker, 2014.

Larman, Craig, and Bas Vodde. *Scaling Lean and Agile Development: Thinking and Organizational Tools for Large-Scale Scrum*. Upper Saddle River, NJ: Addison-Wesley, 2009.

Lewin, K., T. Dembo, L. Festinger, and P. S. Sears. "Levels of Aspiration." in J.M. Hunt. *Personality and the Behavior Disorders*, 1944, 333–378.

Lichtenwalner, Ben. "Dennis Bakke Interview—The Decision Maker Process." Modern Servant Leader (March 12, 2013). https://www.modernservant leader.com/resources/dennis-bakke-interview-decision-maker/.

Linden, Dana. "Incentivize Me, Please." *Forbes* (May 1991).

Lucas, Suzanne. "18 True Tales of Ridiculous Performance Appraisals." Inc.com (September 30, 2018). https://www.inc.com/suzanne-lucas/18-true-tales -of-ridiculous-performance-appraisals.html.

Lucas, Suzanne. "19 (More) Tales of Performance Review Horror." Inc.com (October 22, 2018). https://www.inc.com/suzanne-lucas/19-more-tales-of -performance-review-horror.html.

Maslow, Abraham. *The Farther Reaches of Human Nature*. New York: Penguin Books, 1971.

Maslow, Abraham. *Maslow on Management*. New York: John Wiley & Sons, 1998.

Maslow, Abraham. *Motivation and Personality*. Third Edition. New York: Harper & Row, 1987.

Maslow, Abraham. *Religion, Values, and Peak Experiences*. New York: Penguin Books, 1970.

Maslow, Abraham. *Toward a Psychology of Being*. New York: John Wiley & Sons, 1968.

McFeely, Shane, and Ben Wigert. "This Fixable Problem Costs U.S. Businesses $1 Trillion." Gallup (March 13, 2019). https://www.gallup.com/workplace /247391/fixable-problem-costs-businesses-trillion.aspx.

McGregor, Douglas. *The Human Side of Enterprise*. New York: McGraw-Hill, 1960.

Milgram, Stanley. "Behavioral Study of Obedience." *Journal of Abnormal and Social Psychology* 67, no. 4 (1963): 371–378.

Minnaar, Joost, and Pim de Morree. *Corporate Rebels: Make Work More Fun*. Nederland, B.V.: Corporate Rebels, 2019.

Nissani, Moti. "A Cognitive Reinterpretation of Stanley Milgram's Observations on Obedience to Authority." *American Psychologist* 45, 12 (1990): 1384–1385.

Perez, Matt, Adrian Perez, and Jose Leal. *RADICAL Companies: Without Employees and Bosses*. Pradera Media, 2021.

Pink, Daniel. *Drive: The Surprising Truth About What Motivates Us*. New York: Riverhead Books, 2009.

Plous, Scott. *The Psychology of Judgment and Decision Making*. New York: McGraw-Hill, 1993.

Poole, Henry. "Improving Scrum Team Flow on Digital Service Projects." Medium.com/CivicActions (August 15, 2019). https://medium.com/civicactions/improving-scrum-team-flow-on-digital-service-projects-6723d95eaad8.

Pulse, Tiny. "2018 Employee Retention Report." Tiny Pulse (2018). https://www.tinypulse.com/hubfs/2018%5C%20Employee%5C%20Retention%5C%20Report.pdf.

Quinn, Daniel. *Beyond Civilization: Humanity's Next Great Adventure*. New York: Three Rivers Press, 1999.

Radecki, Dan, PhD, Leonie Hall, Jennifer McCusker, PhD, and Christopher Ancona. *Psychological Safety: The Key to Happy, High-Performing People and Teams*. Academy of Brain-Based Leadership, 2018.

Raveendran, Marlo, Phanish Puranam, and Massimo Warglien. "Division of Labor Through Self-Selection." *Organization Science* (February 2021).

Reichert, Corinne. "Over 80% of Workers Don't Want to Go Back to the Office Full Time, Survey Finds." cnet (March 2021). https://www.cnet.com/health/over-80-of-workers-dont-want-to-go-back-to-the-office-full-time-survey-finds/.

Research, Gartner. "Transform Your Performance Management Strategy." Gartner (2019). https://www.gartner.com/en/human-resources/insights/performance-management.

Ries, Tonia E., and David M. Bersoff. "The Edelman Trust Barometer." Edelman (2021). https://www.edelman.com/trust/2021-trust-barometer.

Robbins, Jim. "Ecopsychology: How Immersion in Nature Benefits Your Health." Yale Environment 360 (January 2020). https://e360.yale.edu/features/ecopsychology-how-immersion-in-nature-benefits-your-health.

Robertson, Brian. "The Holacracy Constitution." Holacracy Constitutions (2021). https://www.holacracy.org/constitution.

Robertson, Brian. *Holacracy: The New Management System for a Rapidly Changing World*. New York: Henry Holt, 2015.

Rogers, Carl, and Richard Farson. *Active Listening*. Mansfield Centre, CT: Martino Publishing, 1957.

Schaufeli, W.B., and A.B. Bakker. "Job Demands, Job Resources, and Their Relationship with Burnout and Engagement: A Multi-Sample Study." *Journal of Organizational Behavior* 25 (2004): 293–315.

Schnurman, Mitchell. "So Long, Boss: As Pandemic Eases, Workers Quit in Record Numbers." *Dallas Morning News* (June 27, 2021). https://www.dallasnews.com/business/2021/06/27/so-long-boss-as-pandemic-eases-workers-quit-in-record-numbers/.

Schwaber, Ken, and Jeff Sutherland. "The Scrum Guide." Scrum Guides (November 2020). https://scrumguides.org/docs/scrumguide/v2020/2020-Scrum-Guide-US.pdf.

Schwarz, Roger. *The Eight Behaviors for Smarter Teams*. Roger Schwarz and Associates, 2011.

Scullen, S., M. Mount, and M. Goff. "Understanding the Latent Structure of Job Performance Ratings." *The Journal of Applied Psychology* 85, no. 6 (2000): 956–970.

Seidman, Dov. *The HOW Report*. LRN, 2016. https://howmetrics.lrn.com/wp/wp-content/uploads/2017/01/HOW_REPORT_5.04.16_finalspreads_b.pdf.

Semler, Ricardo. *The Seven Day Weekend: Changing the Way Work Works*. New York: Penguin, 2004.

Squirrel, Douglas, and Jeffery Fredrick. *Agile Conversations: Transform Your Conversation, Transform Your Organization*. Portland, Oregon: IT Revolution, 2020.

Stayer, Ralph. "How I Learned to Let My Workers Lead." *Harvard Business Review* (November 1990). http://hbr.org/1990/11/how-i-learned-to-let-my-workers-lead.

Taylor, S. E., and S. T. Fiske. "Point of View and Perceptions of Causality." *Journal of Personality and Social Psychology* 32 (1975): 439–445.

Thomson, Peter, Andrew Holm, and Julian Wilson. *500%: How Two Pioneers Transformed Productivity*. London: Magic Sieve Books, 2021.

Threlkeld, Kristy. "Employee Burnout Report: COVID-19's Impact and 3 Strategies to Curb It." Indeed (March 2021). https://www.indeed.com/lead/preventing-employee-burnout-report.

Tower-Clark, Charles. *The Weird CEO: How to Lead in a World Dominated by Artificial Intelligence*. Weird Group Publishing, 2018.

"What Is Employee Engagement and How Do You Improve It?" Gallup. Accessed September 17, 2021. https://www.gallup.com/workplace/285674/improve-employee-engagement-workplace.aspx.

Wikipedia, "The Morning Star Company." Wikipedia.com, last modified September 13, 2021. https://en.wikipedia.org/wiki/The_Morning_Star_Company.

NOTES

Introduction

1. Reichert, "Over 80% of Workers Don't Want to Go Back."
2. Duffy, "Nearly 40% of Workers Would Consider Quitting."
3. Dickler, "'Great Resignation' Gains Steam."
4. Schnurman, "So Long, Boss."
5. Irwin, "Unemployment Is High. Why Are Businesses Struggling to Hire?"
6. Dickler, "'Great Resignation' Gains Steam."
7. Irwin, "Unemployment Is High. Why Are Businesses Struggling to Hire?"
8. Threlkeld, "Employee Burnout Report."
9. Threlkeld, "Employee Burnout Report."
10. Howington, "Survey Explores Varying Attitudes of Millennials and Older Workers."
11. Robbins, "Ecopsychology: How Immersion in Nature Benefits Your Health."
12. Robbins, "Ecopsychology: How Immersion in Nature Benefits Your Health."
13. Birkinshaw, Cohen, and Stach, "Research: Knowledge Workers Are More Productive from Home."
14. Birkinshaw, Cohen, and Stach, "Research: Knowledge Workers Are More Productive from Home."
15. Eisler and Garrick, "Leading the Shift from a Dominator to a Partnership Culture."
16. Eisler, *The Chalice and the Blade*, 121.
17. Schaufeli and Bakker, "Job Demands, Job Resources, and Their Relationship with Burnout and Engagement."
18. Hayes et al., "The Global Study of Engagement."
19. Gallup, "What Is Employee Engagement and How Do You Improve It?"
20. Harter, "Dismal Employee Engagement is a Sign of Global Mismangement."
21. Ries and Bersoff, "The Edelman Trust Barometer."
22. Ries and Bersoff, "The Edelman Trust Barometer."
23. Seidman, *The HOW Report*, 20.
24. Achor et al. "9 Out of 10 People Are Willing to Earn Less Money to Do More Meaningful Work."
25. Achor et al., "9 Out of 10 People Are Willing to Earn Less Money to Do More Meaningful Work."

26. Huang et al., "Reducing Job Insecurity and Increasing Performance Ratings," 853.

27. Khubchandani and Price, "Association of Job Insecurity with Health Risk Factors and Poorer Health in American Workers."

28. Milgram, "Behavioral Study of Obedience," 371–378; Asch, "Effects of Group Pressure on the Modification and Distortion of Judgments," 177–190; Nissani, "A Cognitive Reinterpretation of Stanley Milgram's Observations on Obedience to Authority," 1384–1385.

29. Analytics, "2018 Job Seeker Nation Study: Researching the Candidate-Recruiter Relationship"; Pulse, "2018 Employee Retention Report."

30. McFeely and Wigert, "This Fixable Problem Costs U.S. Businesses $1 Trillion."

31. Eisler, *The Chalice and the Blade*, 14.

32. Seidman, *The HOW Report*, 6.

33. Euromonitor, "Global Major Appliances Brand Rankings."

34. Kirkpatrick, *The No-Limits Enterprise*, Kindle loc. 2159.

35. Hamel and Zanini, *Humanocracy*, 121.

36. Hamel and Zanini, *Humanocracy*, 129.

37. Hamel and Zanini, *Humanocracy*, 130.

38. Hamel and Zanini, *Humanocracy*, 131.

39. Hamel and Zanini, *Humanocracy*, 140.

40. Laloux, *Reinventing Organizations*, 157.

41. Kirkpatrick, *The No-Limits Enterprise*, Kindle loc. 325.

42. Kirkpatrick, *The No-Limits Enterprise*, Kindle loc. 331.

43. Colvine and Branthôme, "Top 50 Tomato Processing Companies Worldwide in 2020."

44. Wikipedia, "The Morning Star Company."

45. Hamel and Zanini, *Humanocracy*, 17.

46. Laloux, *Reinventing Organizations*, 94.

47. Laloux, *Reinventing Organizations*, 95.

48. Hamel and Zanini, *Humanocracy*, 17.

49. Centre for Public Impact, "Buurtzorg: Revolutionising Home Care in the Netherlands."

50. Hamel and Zanini, *Humanocracy*, 18.

51. Hamel and Zanini, *Humanocracy*, 18.

52. Seidman, *The HOW Report*, 6.

53. Seidman, *The HOW Report*, 6.

54. Seidman, *The HOW Report*, 16.

55. Seidman, *The HOW Report*, 7.

56. Seidman, *The HOW Report*, 16.

57. Seidman, *The HOW Report*, 16.

58. Seidman, *The HOW Report*, 23.

59. Seidman, *The HOW Report*, 26.
60. Seidman, *The HOW Report*, 17.
61. Seidman, *The HOW Report*, 6.

Chapter 1

1. Radecki et al., *Psychological Safety*, 59.
2. Radecki et al., *Psychological Safety*, 59.
3. Crumley, "Heterarchy and the Analysis of Complex Societies."
4. Maslow, *Motivation and Personality*, 80.
5. Maslow, *Toward a Psychology of Being*, 38–39.
6. Seidman, *The HOW Report*, 20.
7. Rogers and Farson, *Active Listening*, 21; Maslow, *The Farther Reaches of Human Nature*, 227.
8. Rogers and Farson, *Active Listening*, 21.
9. Maslow, *The Farther Reaches of Human Nature*, 227.

Chapter 2

1. Maslow, *Toward a Psychology of Being*, 168.
2. Maslow, *Maslow on Management*, 56.
3. Minnaar and de Morree, *Corporate Rebels*, Kindle loc. 651.
4. *The Economist*, "Chinese Industry Haier and Higher."
5. Minnaar and de Morree, *Corporate Rebels*, Kindle loc., 592.
6. Minnaar and de Morree, *Corporate Rebels*, Kindle loc., 592.
7. Minnaar and de Morree, *Corporate Rebels*, Kindle loc., 598.
8. Minnaar and de Morree, *Corporate Rebels*, Kindle loc., 651.
9. Hamel and Zanini, *Humanocracy*, 134.
10. Hamel and Zanini, *Humanocracy*, 134.
11. Minnaar and De Morree, *Corporate Rebels*, Kindle loc. 664.
12. Hamel and Zanini, *Humanocracy*, 134.
13. Hamel and Zanini, *Humanocracy*, 135.
14. Minnaar and de Morree, *Corporate Rebels*, Kindle loc., 667.
15. Minnaar and de Morree, *Corporate Rebels*, Kindle loc., 669.
16. Minnaar and de Morree, *Corporate Rebels*, Kindle loc., 672.
17. Schwaber and Sutherland, "The Scrum Guide."
18. Semler, *The Seven Day Weekend*, i.
19. Kirkpatrick, *The No-Limits Enterprise*, Kindle loc., 1129 .
20. Semler, *The Seven Day Weekend*, iii.
21. Raveendran et al., *Division of Labor Through Self-Selection*, 2, 4.
22. Seidman, *The HOW Report*, 22.
23. Fishman, "Engines of Democracy."

24. Fishman, "Engines of Democracy."
25. Seidman, *The HOW Report*, 16.
26. Seidman, *The HOW Report*, 16.
27. Raveendran et al., *Division of Labor Through Self-Selection*, 3–4.
28. Robertson, *Holacracy Constitution*.
29. Robertson, *Holacracy*, 199.
30. Robertson, *Holacracy*, 44.
31. Robertson, *Holacracy*, 39.
32. Fishman, "Engines of Democracy."
33. Fishman, "Engines of Democracy."
34. Fishman, "Engines of Democracy."
35. Fishman, "Engines of Democracy."
36. Fishman, "Engines of Democracy."
37. Fishman, "Engines of Democracy."
38. Fishman, "Engines of Democracy."
39. Fishman, "Engines of Democracy."
40. Glass, *Software Runaways*, 57.
41. Glass, *Software Runaways*, 68.
42. Larman and Vodde, *Scaling Lean and Agile Development*, 157.
43. Larman and Vodde, *Scaling Lean and Agile Development*, 154–155.
44. Andy Hawks and Aaron Pava, online interview, February 10, 2021. This story was relayed to the author during interviews he conducted with CivicActions for this book. The particular details and statistics surrounding this work are confidential and are not included in this book.

Chapter 3

1. Stayer, "How I Learned to Let My Workers Lead."
2. Fishman, "Engines of Democracy."
3. Damani, "Pods: A Step Towards Self-Management."
4. Widely attributed to Peter Senge.
5. Thomson, Holm, and Wilson, *500%*, 56.
6. Thomson, Holm, and Wilson, *500%*, 57–58.
7. Thomson, Holm, and Wilson, *500%*, 57–58.
8. Thomson, Holm, and Wilson, *500%*, 104.
9. Holm, "Fractal Model."
10. Holm, "From Time to Value."
11. Perez, Perez, and Leal, *RADICAL Companies*, 240.
12. Perez, Perez, and Leal, *RADICAL Companies*, 5.
13. Perez, Perez, and Leal, *RADICAL Companies*, 8.
14. Perez, Perez, and Leal, *RADICAL Companies*, 17.

15. Kirkpatrick, *The No-Limits Enterprise*, Kindle loc. 553.
16. Perez, Perez, and Leal, *RADICAL Companies*, 254.
17. Perez, Perez, and Leal, *RADICAL Companies*, 57.
18. Perez, Perez, and Leal, *RADICAL Companies*, 15.
19. Perez, Perez, and Leal, *RADICAL Companies*, 20.
20. Perez, Perez, and Leal, *RADICAL Companies*, 21.
21. De Morree, "This Company Democratically Elects its CEO Every Single Year."
22. De Morree, "This Company Democratically Elects its CEO Every Single Year."
23. De Morree, "This Company Democratically Elects Its CEO Every Single Year."
24. De Morree, "This Company Democratically Elects its CEO Every Single Year."
25. De Morree, "This Company Democratically Elects its CEO Every Single Year."
26. De Morree, "This Company Democratically Elects its CEO Every Single Year."
27. Minnaar and de Morree, *Corporate Rebels*, Kindle loc. 1589.
28. Arnold, "Why We Have Replaced Leadership Elections."
29. Arnold, "Why We Have Replaced Leadership Elections."
30. Arnold, "Why We Have Replaced Leadership Elections."
31. Lichtenwalner, "Dennis Blake Interview - The Decision Maker Process."
32. Lichtenwalner, "Dennis Blake Interview - The Decision Maker Process."
33. Lichtenwalner, "Dennis Blake Interview - The Decision Maker Process."
34. Laloux, *Reinventing Organizations*, 125.
35. Robertson, *Holacracy*, 8.
36. Robertson, *Holacracy*, 9.
37. Robertson, *Holacracy*, 38.
38. Robertson, *Holacracy*, 65.
39. Deutschman, "The Fabric of Creativity."
40. Deutschman, "The Fabric of Creativity."

Chapter 4

1. Consultancy.uk, "UK Employees Losing Faith in Annual Performance Management Cycles."
2. Gartner, "Transform Your Performance Management Strategy."
3. Scullen, Mount, and Goff, "Understanding the Latent Structure of Job Performance Ratings."
4. Lucas, "18 True Tales of Ridiculous Performance Appraisals."
5. Lucas, "18 True Tales of Ridiculous Performance Appraisals."
6. Lucas, "19 (More) Tales of Performance Review Horror."
7. Lucas, "18 True Tales of Ridiculous Performance Appraisals."
8. Lucas, "18 True Tales of Ridiculous Performance Appraisals."
9. Lucas, "18 True Tales of Ridiculous Performance Appraisals."
10. McGregor, *The Human Side of Enterprise,* Kindle loc. 1167.

11. Maslow, *The Farther Reaches of Human Nature*, 24.
12. Deci, Koestner, and Ryan. "A Meta-Analytic Review of Experiments," 658.
13. Maslow, *Toward a Psychology of Being*, 6.
14. Deci, Koestner, and Ryan. "A Meta-Analytic Review of Experiments," 659.
15. Pink, *Drive*, 59.
16. Kohn, *Punished By Rewards*, 42.
17. Kohn, *Punished By Rewards*, 43.
18. Kohn, *Punished By Rewards*, 43.
19. Deci, "Effects of Externally Mediated Rewards on Intrinsic Motivation," 105.
20. Kohn, *Punished By Rewards*, 45.
21. Kohn, *Punished By Rewards*, 48.
22. Kohn, *Punished By Rewards*, 69.
23. Deci, "Effects of Externally Mediated Rewards on Intrinsic Motivation," 114.
24. Deci, "Effects of Externally Mediated Rewards on Intrinsic Motivation," 114.
25. Kohn, *Punished By Rewards*, 70.
26. Kohn, *Punished By Rewards*, 70.
27. Bruner and Postman, "On the Perception of Incongruity."
28. Plous, *The Psychology of Judgment and Decision Making*, 15–16
29. Plous, *The Psychology of Judgment and Decision Making*, 15.
30. Taylor and Fiske, "Point of View and Perceptions of Causality."
31. Plous, *The Psychology of Judgment and Decision Making*, 178
32. Plous, *The Psychology of Judgment and Decision Making*, 179.
33. Plous, *The Psychology of Judgment and Decision Making*, 179.
34. Plous, *The Psychology of Judgment and Decision Making*, 145.
35. Plous, *The Psychology of Judgment and Decision Making*, 151.
36. Plous, *The Psychology of Judgment and Decision Making*, 151.
37. Hamel and Zanini, *Humanocracy*, 123.
38. Hamel and Zanini, *Humanocracy*, 124.
39. Hamel and Zanini, *Humanocracy*, 125.
40. Thomson, Holm, and Wilson, *500%*, 104.
41. Hamel and Zanini, *Humanocracy*, 132.
42. Hamel and Zanini, *Humanocracy*, 135.
43. Minnaar and de Morree, *Corporate Rebels*, Kindle loc. 669.
44. Hamel and Zanini, *Humanocracy*, 132.
45. Minnaar and de Morree, *Corporate Rebels*, Kindle loc. 1589.
46. Deming, *The Essential Deming*, 27.
47. Deming, *The Essential Deming*, 27.
48. Deming, *The New Economics*, 28.
49. Linden, "Incentivize Me, Please," 208.
50. Hornung, "Why We Should Not Punish Intrinsic Motivation."

51. Hannah, "'My Boss Lets Me Set My Own Salary.'"
52. Tower-Clark, *The Weird CEO*, 122
53. McFeely and Wigert, "This Fixable Problem Costs U.S. Businesses $1 Trillion."

Chapter 5

1. Maslow, *Toward a Psychology of Being*, 37, 40.
2. Maslow, *Toward a Psychology of Being*, 168.
3. Maslow, *Toward a Psychology of Being*, 39.
4. Poole, "Improving Scrum Team Flow on Digital Service Projects."
5. Seidman, *The HOW Report*, 20.
6. Robertson, *Holacracy*, 70.
7. Robertson, *Holacracy*, 70.
8. Seidman, *The HOW Report*, 23.

Chapter 6

1. Argyris, *Organizational Traps*, 63.
2. Argyris, *Overcoming Organizational Defenses*, 13.
3. Argyris, *Organizational Traps*, 64.
4. Seidman, *The HOW Report*, 12.
5. Seidman, *The HOW Report*, 12.
6. Schwarz, *The Eight Behaviors for Smarter Teams*.
7. Lewin et al., "Levels of Aspiration," in Hunt, *Personality and the Behavior Disorders*, 333–378.
8. Argyris, *Overcoming Organizational Defenses*, 120.
9. Thomson, Holm, and Wilson, *500%*, 77.
10. Thomson, Holm, and Wilson, *500%*, 77.

Conclusion

1. Seidman, *The HOW Report*, 20.
2. Seidman, *The HOW Report*, 16.
3. Seidman, *The HOW Report*, 6.
4. Dawkins, *The Selfish Gene*.
5. Quinn, *Beyond Civilization: Humanity's Next Great Adventure*, 7.
6. Maslow, *Toward a Psychology of Being*, 31.
7. Maslow, *Religion, Values, and Peak Experiences*, 92–93.
8. Maslow, *Toward a Psychology of Being*, 40, 43.
9. Maslow, *Religion, Values, and Peak Experiences*, 94.
10. Maslow, *Toward a Psychology of Being*, 130.
11. Maslow, *Toward a Psychology of Being*, 31–32.

12. Maslow, *The Farther Reaches of Human Nature*, 243.
13. Maslow, *Toward a Psychology of Being*, 86.
14. Maslow, *Toward a Psychology of Being*, 32.

Acknowledgments

1. King, *On Writing*, 73.

INDEX

Note: Figures are indicated with *f*; tables are indicated with *t*.

A

Actively disengaged employees, xv. *See also* Disengagement
Ad hoc leadership teams
  defined, 11
  at Nearsoft, 53–57
Advice process
  at AES Corporation, 63–65
  defined, 11, 62, 63
  at Haufe-umantis, 48, 65–66
AES Corporation, 63–65
Agile Conversations: Transform Your Conversations, Transform Your Culture, 116
Airplane instruments manufacturer
  description of, 9*t*
  fractal organization at, 12, 48–53
  pay system at, 12, 87–88, 89
  spontaneous candid vulnerability at, 118–119
Allan, Graham, 20, 72
Allocation, autonomy of
  defined, 4, 26
  inspired employees and, 104–105
  job fairs for, 28
  motivation and, 4, 29, 30, 104
  results of, 30
  self-selection of tasks, 26–27
  the *what* and *who*, 3, 4*f*, 18
Anchoring, 85–86
Annual performance appraisals
  dissatisfaction with, 75–77
  dominator hierarchies and, xvi, 75, 77
  first impressions and, 85–86
  myth of necessity and, 77, 78–83
  myth of objectivity and, 77, 83–87
Appliance manufacturer

description of, 9*t*, 15–18
microenterprises at, xxi–xxii, 15–18, 106
pay system at, 87–88, 89
Argyris, Chris, 110, 111, 113, 114, 117
Arnold, Hermann, 60–61, 62
Aspiration diversity, 117
Autonomy. *See also* Team autonomy
  defined, 3–5
  as human need, 15, 97, 98
  questions for reflection, 41–42
  six dimensions of, 4*f*, 18–19
Autonomy of allocation
  deficiency gratification of, 104–105
  defined, 4, 26
  intrinsic motivation and, 4, 29, 30, 104
  job fairs for, 28
  results of, 31
  self-selection of tasks, 26–27
  the *what* and *who*, 3, 4*f*, 18
Autonomy of practice
  defined, 4, 19
  at Haufe-umantis, 20–21
  the *how*, 3, 4*f*, 18
  regulations and, 19
  Scrum and, 21–22
  at TIM Group, 20
Autonomy of role
  explanation of, 4, 30
  in a Holacracy, 32–33, 68–69
  job crafting, 30–31
  at Nearsoft, 31–32
  team autonomy and, 3, 4*f*, 18
Autonomy of schedule
  at CivicActions, 23–24
  defined, 4
  four-day week, 26
  at Haufe-umantis, 24–25
  objections to, 22–23
  at Semco Partners, 25–26

Microenterprises
    defined, xxi–xxii, 15
    at Haier, xxi–xxii, 15–18, 106
Mentors
    onboarding buddies, 12, 70–73
    in peer pods, 12, 47
Mindset
    advice, 66
    dominator, 130
    freedom-based, 70–71
Mistakes, admitting
    biggest fail of the week, 13, 116, 117
    as espoused routine, 112
    spontaneous candid vulnerability and,
        118–121
Mistrust
    dominator hierarchies and, xviii, 3, 15
    "The Great Resignation" and, xviii
Mohan, Pranay, 29, 30, 102, 104, 106
Morning Star (tomato processor)
    description of, 10t
    as radically collaborative organization,
        xxi
    zero bosses at, xxii–xxiii
Motivation, intrinsic
    autonomy of allocation and, 27–30
    extrinsic rewards and, 79, 81–83
Myth of necessity
    control of compensation and, 77
    rewards and performance, 78–83
    Theory X and, 22–23, 78–80, 82
Myth of objectivity
    control of compensation and, 77
    studies illustrating, 83–87

N
Nature, time in, xiv
Nearshore consulting agencies, 31
Nearsoft
    accountability at, 25
    advice process at, 65
    autonomy of role at, 31–32
    brief description of, 10t, 31
    firings at, 25, 59–60
    leadership teams at, 48, 53–57
    meeting prompts at, 102
    motto, 70
    onboarding at, 70–71

Necessity, myth of, 77, 78–83
Needs, human, 97–98, 127
No-Limits Enterprise, The, xxiii, 55
No secrets rule, 56, 57

O
Objectivity, myth of
    control of compensation and, 77
    studies illustrating, 83–87
Offshoring, 54
Onboarding, 12, 70–73
Outcome teams
    advantages of, 38
    bubbles, 11, 38
    component teams versus, 35–37
    generalists on, 37
    group assembly in, 34–35, 37
    priorities, purpose, and, 39
Outdoors, spending time in the, xiv
Ownership, sense of, 51–52

P
Pair programming
    defined, 4, 11
    at Pivotal Labs, viii, 59
    at TIM Group, 20
Parker, Andy, 72
Pava, Aaron, 23, 24, 100, 103, 105, 120,
    121
Pay, control of. *See* Devolution of
    compensation
Pay, self-managed
    defined, 12, 91
    at GrantTree, 92
    at Pod Group, 92–93
Pay system, Deming
    description of, 12, 89–90
    radical collaborators and, 6
    at Viisi fintech company, 10t, 90–91
Peer pods
    building trust with, 103–104
    defined, 12, 103
    mentoring in, 12, 47
Perez, Matt, 54, 55–56, 57, 60
Performance appraisals
    anchoring effect and, 85–86
    dissatisfaction with, 75–77
    dominator hierarchies and, xvi, 75, 77

eight behaviors and, 114
at TIM Group, 115–116

U

Undiscussable issues, discussing, 114,
 120
Unemployment, voluntary, xiii–xiv
Unilateral control, 110, 111, 114

V

Velora, 39–40
Veterans Affairs administration, 40–41
Viisi
  Deming Pay System at, 90–91
  general description of 10*t*, 90
Vodde, Bas, 36–37, 38
Voluntary unemployment, xi

W

W.L. Gore
  advice process at, 65
  brief description of, 10*t*, 45
  onboarding at, 12, 72
  as pioneer, 10*t*, 45, 109
  TIM Group and, 44–46
What and *who* of work
  as autonomy of allocation, 3, 4*f*, 18
  as deficiency gratification, 104–105
  explanation of, 4, 26
  intrinsic motivation and, 4, 29, 30, 104
  job fairs, 28
  results of choosing, 30–31
  self-selection of tasks, 26–27
Where and *when* to do the work
  as autonomy of schedule, 3, 4*f*, 18
  at CivicActions, 23–24
  four-day week, 26
  at Haufe-umantis, 24–25
  objections to choosing, 22–23
  at Semco Partners, 25–26
White, Matthew, xiv
Wilson, Julian, 49
Work/life balance
  autonomy of schedule and, 22–26
  balance scores and, 12, 99–101
  four-day week and, 26
  importance of, xiv

Workplace culture
  deficiency gratification and, 95–96
  dominator hierarchies and, xvii–xviv,
    130–131
  ego-driven behavior and, 95
  freedom-based, 70–71

X

Xinchu microenterprise, at Haier, xxii

Z

Zamora, Nyx, 32, 59, 102
Zanini, Michele, 88
Zero bosses. *See also* Managerial
  devolution
  everyone as CEO, 15, 89
  fractal organizational model and, 50
  Holacracy and, 66–68
  at Morning Star, xxii–xxiii, 10*t*
  at Nearsoft, 10*t*, 55
  at W.L. Gore, 72
Zero-fund entrepreneurial support
  program, 89
Zhang Ruimin, xxii, 15–16, 88, 89

ABOUT THE AUTHOR

Matt K. Parker is a writer, speaker, researcher, and third-generation programmer. Over the last two decades, he's played a variety of roles in the software industry, including developer, manager, director, and global head of engineering.

He has specialized in hyperiterative software practices for the last decade and is currently researching the experience of radically collaborative software makers.

He lives in a small village in Connecticut with his wife and three children. You can contact him by visiting mattkparker.com.